The Illustrated History of
COVENTRY'S SUBURBS
to the end of the 20th Century

First published in Great Britain in 2003 by
The Breedon Books Publishing Company Limited

This edition published in Great Britain in 2018
by DB Publishing, an imprint of JMD Media Ltd

ISBN 978-1-78091-571-5

CONTENTS

ACKNOWLEDGEMENTS

May I thank the following for supplying information: Coventry Local Studies in the Central Library, with special thanks to Karen Berry, Andrew Mealey and the staff; Coventry Archives; David Morgan; John Ashby; Gordon Cowley; Albert Peck and also the many people and sources mentioned in the text.

Special thanks go to Coventry Library Services, Local Studies for supplying over half of the illustrations for the book. The remaining illustrations were supplied by John Ashby, David Morgan, Gordon Cowley, June Manley, *Coventry Evening Telegraph*, Trevor Pring, Jack Mellor, J. Priestley, June Raven, Cliff Barlow, Frank Scotland, Joseph York, Roger Bailey and the David McGrory Collection. Also many thanks to Kathleen and Susan Spragg for use of copyright Florence Weston drawings currently held in the Coventry and Warwickshire Collection.

I would also like to thank Rupert Harding for his hard work in the initial stages of this project.

CCL: Coventry City Library, Coventry and Warwickshire Collection.

Introduction

The earliest mention of any district of Coventry is probably found in the Cartulary of Coventry Priory, in which we are informed that the monks held an ancient book, which had belonged to Leofric and Godiva, in which the property of the monks as given by Leofric was listed. The book claimed that Sow (Walsgrave-on-Sowe) was held by the church, even in the reign of King Edgar who died in 975, making this the oldest claim to a district in the Coventry area. The earliest existing claimed copy of Leofric's charter to the priory (most are forgeries) dates from 1267 and lists 24 lordships around Coventry that he gave to the monks, and 'a moiety of the town, in which the church itself is situate.' The only mention in the charter of an actual district by name is part of Sow (Walsgrave).

One of the earliest reliable charters referring to a Coventry district comes from Ranulf Gernon, Earl of Chester, who by licence of Roger de Clinton, Bishop of Coventry (1129–1149) built a chapel at Wyken, for the 'advantage of poor people.' Around the same time Ranulf built another chapel at Allesley. A further charter of Ranulf dated between 1144 and 1153 tells us of Leofric's bequest 'aforetime', presumably the moiety and manors, including part of Sow, and begins, 'Ranulf, Earl of Chester, to all his Frenchmen and Englishmen... Be it known unto you that I have granted and given to God and St Mary, and to Laurence the Prior, and the Convent of the monks of Coventry, my rights which belonged to them aforetime.' The charter gives the church all the chapels without the town and all parochial rights and tithes of Anesti (Ansty), Sulftona (Shilton), Wica (Wyken), Bilneyae (Binley), Witeleia (Whitley), Pynnleia (Pinley), Stoca (Stoke), Stivichala (Stivichall), Eccleshale (Exhall), Folkeshulla (Foleshill), Keresleia (Keresley), Watburleia (Whoberley), Spanna (Spon) and Bisselia (Bisseley). These rights are verified by Bishop Gerard la Pucelle in 1185 with that of Allesley.

An inquisition taken in 1349 of the property of Coventry Priory following the death of Prior William from the plague shows that the monks had lost a great many of the manors endowed on them. Their remaining lands and properties lay mainly on the north side of Coventry at Harnall, Whitmoor, Hawkesbury, Newland, Radford, Exhall, Keresley, Coundon, Willenhall and Sowe. It was noted that year that the two watermills and a windmill in Radford were abandoned. Their operators had either fled or died of the plague; the prior's tenants at Radford, Keresley, Coundon, Willenhall and Exhall had been largely wiped out as the Black Death rampaged through the districts.

In 1451 King Henry VI, who for over two and a half years based his court in Coventry, granted the city special status. Coventry and the villages of Ansty, Asthill, Biggin, Caludon, Exhall, Foleshill, Harnall, Henley-le-Wood-End, Horwell, Keresley, Pinley, Stoke, Radford, Whitley, Whoberley, Wyken and part of Sow (Walsgrave) and Stivichall were united together to form a county in themselves. Thus the city and county of Coventry was born, and it endured until 1842 when lawsuits about loss of electoral rights and high rates led to an act of Parliament depriving the city of county status.

The city limits were redefined and the city spread. This was helped by the enclosure of much of the Lammas and Michaelmas lands, which had belonged to the freemen of the city and for centuries has formed a barrier to its expansion. In 1890, Earlsdon, Radford and the Red Lane district were taken into the city boundaries. In 1899 further extensions were made taking in parts of Stoke and Foleshill. In 1926 the Coventry Corporation purchased the Stoneleigh Estate, which allowed it to expand its boundary in 1928, taking into the city parts of Foleshill, Stoke, Whitley, Cheylesmore, Stoneleigh, Canley, Westwood Heath, Tile Hill, Eastern Green and Allesley. Further extensions came in 1932 with the addition of Walsgrave, Wyken, Willenhall, Binley, Stivichall and parts of Keresley and Exhall. The remaining sections of villages such as Keresley, previously under Meriden, were taken into the city in the early 1960s and thus the city of Coventry swallowed up the small villages and hamlets which for centuries had been scattered around it in open countryside.

ALLESLEY

The earliest recorded version of the name dates back to 1176 and is recorded as 'Alleslega,' which means Aella's clearing. The Saxon personal name Aella was most common during the 9th century and in this case it has been suggested that it could have been the name of a local landowner. There is however a possible alternative explanation. In 867 an army led by Aella held York and much of the realm after a prolonged period of warfare. This army set up camps as it moved through the realm, so could the clearing at Allesley be one of Aella's marching camps set within the woodland of Arden? Interestingly there does appear to have been a defensive encampment halfway up Staircase Lane, a large, round, raised field called the Roundabout Close, which forces the lane out of line to follow its edge. However, this is believed to have been a prehistoric fortified encampment. Staircase Lane in the past has also been the find site of petrified wood from an ancient forest. Here in 1831 a complete tree base was discovered, measuring some 12ft long and 5ft around. It is said that in the same pits fossils are found and once a live toad was discovered within solid rock.

In around 1150 Ranulf Gernon, Earl of Chester, had a chapel built in Allesley, under licence from the Bishop of Coventry. This may reflect the growth of the village, with its connection to the nearby castle, which is traditionally believed to have been built around this time. This does make some sense, since Ranulf Gernon was a castle-builder and had the first Coventry Castle built during the period known as the Baron's War.

Allesley Castle has always been a problem — was it a castle or a fortified mansion? We may never know the answer. The site of the 'castle' was on and around the site of the present Allesley Hall. Its occupier in the 1930s, Dr John Orton, kept a scrapbook in which is related this story from an unknown source. It states:

> In the turbulent days of King Stephen in 1146, 'Black Roger,' the Baron of Maxstoke, incensed that he could not marry the daughter of Sir Fulk Hastings, attacked Allesley Castle, slaughtering its occupants and burning it to the ground. Will Braynes, the seneschal, is said to have escaped, but was pursued and eventually murdered near the Pack-Horse Gatehouse of the castle. The Old Stone House on the Birmingham Road is reputed to be a remnant of that gatehouse and tales were once told of a man in armour who haunts the site.

It is possible that a temporary castle stood here during the Baron's War in King Stephen's reign (1135–1154) but the Hasting family did not hold the manor until the latter part of the reign of Henry III, who died in 1272. As for 'Black Roger', history is silent. The story may therefore contain a grain of truth, along with later additions.

Most historical sources agree that a residence was built here by the Hasting family (who also held Fillongley Castle) in the early 14th century. They certainly held it in 1305 because the Stoneleigh Leger Book records an agreement between John de Hasting and Abbot John of Stoneleigh to exchange land to add to the deer park in exchange for stopping men from pasturing their cattle on the abbot's

Early 19th-century engraving of Allesley Hall and Park. (CCL)

land below Broad Lane. Hasting completed his 400-acre deer park stretching from Allesley to Broad Lane and the family held the manor until 1389. What the Hasting residence was like we do not know, but John de Hasting was a powerful lord and the deer park would suggest a house of some size. There is a reference from 1583 stating that Robert Fitch left among his possessions 'the site of the late Castle of Allesley.' In 1962 children digging in the dried-up moat unearthed 15th-century decorated floor tiles, bearing animals and *fleur de lys*.

In Dugdale's *Warwickshire* of 1817 Dr Thomas states:

> *... there still remains a piece of an ancient castle, which seems to have been double moated about; in the innermost moat was found a well, steined about with stone five feet deep, which being cleaned, proves an admirable spring, and serves the house and offices. By the side of the well there was found a stone trough, with five several holes with bits of leaded pipes in them, which formerly conveyed the water five several ways.*

It seems likely that John de Hasting did indeed build himself a small castle in Allesley.

Dugdale says that Allesley Castle passed by marriage from the Hasting family to Sir William Beauchamp, son of the Earl of Warwick, then to the Nevilles and from them to Sir Henry Compton, who owned it in 1640. The Civil War period may have seen the destruction of the castle, much like Caludon, or it may have been demolished by Thomas Flynt, who built a new house in front of the castle site in 1660. Flynt died in 1670, passing the estate onto his wife, Martha, who was pregnant. The child inherited the estate at the age of 21 but died three weeks later. Martha re-inherited, sold the estate and left.

Allesley Village in 1910 with the Rainbow Inn on the left. (CCL)

In 1692 Henry Neale (whose wife was related to Cromwell) purchased the estate. Some say it was he who built the new entrance to the hall, creating Allesley Hall Drive. Tradition, however, states that Neale, wishing to build the new drive, borrowed money to plant an avenue of elms looking towards the spires of Coventry. He proposed to excavate the ground between the trees to create a drive running from the old road, but it is said he was distracted by being persuaded to stand as a Whig MP for Coventry. The money for the drive was supposedly lost at the election and the work was never completed.

In 1713 Henry's eldest son John fought and lost the same seat, although he eventually won it in 1722. It was said that the Neales were fast-living, hard-drinking gamblers and part of the estate was lost at the card table. The Rectory of Allesley was also said to have been sold off to pay election debts.

Captain Joseph Neale of the Horse Guards, John's brother, requested that these words be placed on his grave in Allesley church:

Ah! Poor Joe Neale!
Who loved good ale!
For want of good ale!
Here lies poor Joe Neale!

It is said that the family found the verse embarrassing and had the stone shortened during the restoration of 1863 leaving only the first line.

After 1812 the Neales left the hall and for 30 years rented it to James Beck, a Coventry bank owner. The 1841 census shows that a 60-year-old Beck shared the hall with 10 female relatives and his grandson. There were 11 servants. The building later became a boys' boarding school, founded as the Midland School in 1848 by Thomas Wyles, and became Allesley Park College in 1861. It was then occupied by Lieutenant-Colonel Francis Newdigate Kevitt Rotherham in 1896 and in 1908 it came into the hands of William Issac Iliffe, founder of the *Midland Daily Telegraph*, the forerunner of the *Coventry Evening Telegraph*. Iliffe rebuilt the hall in 1910 and after his son's death in 1937 it was left to the city. Since then Allesley Hall has been used as a convalescent home, an orthopaedic hospital, a leisure centre with a golf course and a nursing home.

The rectors of Allesley's church of All Saints have occasionally been colourful, but not as colourful as William Warde, who after many warnings for misbehaviour was brought to court in 1638. There he was charged with frequenting ale houses in Allesley and Coventry, drunkenness during the service, playing ninepins with a local butcher on a Sunday while drunk, fighting a cobbler in an ale-house yard and lastly threatening to kill Mrs Hemmingham's dog while brandishing a knife. Men of greater religious devotion to God and the village were the Brees. The Revd Thomas Bree became rector in 1749 and Brees looked after the flock until the last, the Revd William Bree, who was also Archdeacon of Coventry, died in 1917. Interestingly the first Revd Thomas Bree asked to be buried on the north side of the church in 1778, as a protest against an old superstition relating to the Devil's side.

There is a short description of passing through Allesley on Dan Claridge's stagecoach in 1878:

> *Leaving Coventry by the new Holyhead Road, Allesley Church peeps upward among the trees. At the top of the hill the site of the castle of the Hastings family on rising ground near the Hall is discernible; on the eastern slope of which are the Butts where our volunteers delight in scoring bulls-eyes. Crossing the Sherbourne we soon rejoin the old line of road where a superannuated Toll-house formerly kept watch over the junction and we rattle into Allesley with the sound of the horn.*

The previously mentioned rifle butts were created by the Coventry Rifle Volunteers in 1859. Here for the defence of the realm the volunteers practiced their rifle shooting against earthen butts, which they dug themselves. The tollhouse used to stand on the junction of the Holyhead Road (built between 1828 and 1831) and the Allesley Old Road (near the present Tollgate pub). The building stood at the fork of the roads and controlled traffic by toll through two white gates. The tollhouse stood until the road was widened in around 1931. Behind the tollhouse once stood an enormous barn, known locally as the Tithe Barn. In the mid-19th century a farm labourer hung himself in the barn and was buried in the nearby road just before the tollhouse. This was because it was believed that a suicide would rise as a ghost and haunt the area. By burying him in the road near a junction it was believed the spirit would stay trapped, not knowing which way to go.

Other superstitions continued in Allesley, such as remnants of ancient well worship, for the Revd William Bree wrote in 1829 of Dudley's Spring in the village: 'it has long been held in estimation among the lower orders for foretelling, as they believe, the dearness of corn, and many old people have been in the habit of watching its operations, and placing much faith in them.'

Our stage-coach passenger of 1878 continues:

> *We neither stayed at the 'Rainbow' which still does business, nor at the 'White Lion' the sign of which has disappeared ... the 'Old Inn' where Coventry citizens in olden times held picnics and consumed cheesecakes, has been metamorphosed into a double dwelling house. Close by is the school, a newly erected building and nearly opposite, the site of the old stocks.*

The Rainbow is still probably one of the best-known inns in Coventry. It has stood since 1680 and was said to have originally been a meeting place for those engaged in cock-fighting. The inn was owned by the Revd Thomas Bree of Allesley and the Revd William Bree of Coleshill from 1798 and continued in the family until it was sold to pay death duties in 1949. Also sold was 'Gable End', which was built in 1700 and originally called 'The Pannier'. It is said that in the 18th century this was one of the finest bowling greens in England.

'Pinket's Booth', built in around 1630, was also once an inn called the Royal Oak. This was probably Richard Pinket's alehouse, which was suppressed in 1635 for selling a quart of ale for one penny. The suppression was dropped three years later for good conduct. The White Lion, renowned for its cheesecake, is now called Lion House. It was originally a large coaching inn. Another popular inn nearby, now a farmhouse, was the Windmill.

Allesley village has many original buildings still standing, including the beautiful Stone House which appears to date from the late 16th century. It was said to have been sold by the lord of the manor in 1608 to William Clark, although above the doorway are the initials W.W.O. It has been suggested that this should be W.W.C. for William Clark and his son William, but the use of combined initials normally indicates a man and wife. The Stone House is said to be haunted by a man in armour, a grey lady, a stagecoach and a headless horseman.

Another interesting building in the area, recently converted into a pub-restaurant, is the old Paybody Eye Hospital. The building is said to date back to 1600, when on 30 September George Pooler, a poor man of Allesley, was given permission to build a cottage on waste ground east of the church. The cottage was sold to Richard Ebourne, a baker, in 1629 and his son, also called Richard, built the main house onto the original cottage. Richard's bake-ovens still survived in 1991.

The Ebournes left the house in 1747 and let the building to tenants. For a period during the 19th century it became a boys' boarding school. In the late 1880s the Lancaster family bought and moved into the property and in 1912 it was sold to Henry Bennett, owner of Coventry Opera House. In 1929 it became a convalescent home, after which it was presented to the Crippled Children's Guild by Thomas Paybody. In 1938 it became an orthopaedic hospital, then the Paybody Eye Hospital.

A notorious incident concerning body-snatchers took place in Allesley at the end of February 1830 when the *Coventry Herald* reported that a person going to ring the six o'clock bell had discovered that the grave of Joseph Arnett, aged 70, had been disturbed and the body was gone. Suspicion fell on two strangers who had been drinking at the Rainbow public house the previous afternoon, who had had a large box made, which they said was to be a tool-chest. On Saturday evening some boards were found under a hedge and, supposing the body-snatchers would return, 10 villagers sat up all night to watch the churchyard. However, all remained quiet. On Sunday, a Mr Hollick, who had been searching the hedges and ditches, found a sack containing a human body in a gorse bush about a quarter of a mile from Allesley. Again villagers kept watch during the night but no one came, so on Monday morning the sack was taken to the White Lion and the body identified as Joseph Arnett. It was later recommitted to the churchyard.

Allesley Tollgate from the Allesley Old Road, photographed in around 1865. The Tollgate pub now stands near the site. (CCL)

Since its days as a village Allesley has been encroached upon in the 20th century, and despite retaining the feel of a village in the high street it is very much part of Coventry. It does, however, retain some of its lovely open countryside, part of which was swallowed by the Coundon Wedge Road, laid out in the 1980s. Other parts of Allesley include the Mount Nod area, built over during the 1950s and 60s. Much of the land here was originally part of the hall's deer park, which later became farmland. Mount Nod Farm is noted for having a very powerful spring beneath it, which was capable of pouring out thousands of gallons of water each day. The spring may be very significant, since many ancient sacred places were springs dedicated to various deities. Springs on top of mounts were even more significant: with this in mind the name 'Nod' can be directly connected to the Celtic god Nuada of the Silver Hand, later changed by the Romans to Noden or simply Nod. Shrines to Nod have been found around the country, usually on high places and often associated with springs.

Other built up parts of Allesley are Eastern Green and Pickford Green. The origins of Eastern Green are unknown and it does not appear in the records until 1528. Pickford and Pickford Green take their name from the 'Pikeford' of 1362, which was a ford that crossed the brook, which at that time may have been larger and known to contain pike, probably drawn there by smaller fish looking for food particles in the water disturbed by people fording the stream. The ford site is now Pickford Bridge, which has disappeared under the Birmingham road and was the site in September 1770 of the robbery of the *Liverpool Dilligence* (a coach) by three mounted highwaymen.

Hawkes End is first mentioned in 1389 as the 'Hauokestiestrete', meaning the hawk street. It became 'Hawxtye end' in 1533 and basically refers to a path or place noted for its hawks, which were valued creatures until the 17th century. In the past the only buildings in the area were Hawkes End Farm and a mill and boathouse known as Allesley Mill. In the 1930s a small number of houses and bungalows were built above the farm.

The Stone House, one of Allesley village's finest buildings, photographed in 1914. The lane in front of the building is traditionally said to be the original track to Allesley Castle. (CCL)

Further Reading

Sir William Dugdale, *Warwickshire*, 1817, revised.

Allesley Park Residents Association booklets, *Focus*, articles by David Sheppard.

T.W. Whitley, *The Parliamentary Representation of the City of Coventry*, 1894.

Various newspapers and cuttings, Local Studies, Coventry Library.

W.E. Palmer and W. Parkinson, *Allesley in Times Past*, 1984.

BAGINTON

Baginton appears as Badechitone in the Domesday Book of 1086, the name meaning 'the settlement of Beders' or 'Beadeca's people'. Despite this early mention of the area and its mill in the Domesday Book, Baginton's history stretches much further back. The site has been occupied since prehistoric times. In 1928, a member of the Coventry Archaeological Research Society, accompanied by Mr F. Shotton, a Cambridge University-based archaeologist, set about proving the existence of prehistoric man in Warwickshire. They explored the newly opened gravel pits at Baginton looking for Palaeolithic scrapers.

Baginton Hall as it looked in the early 1800s.

Mr J. Edwards, the amateur archaeologist, wrote of their exploits in the *Coventry Standard* in 1936:

We were successful in finding Palaeolithic implements and we have eight specimens of the old Stone Age. But while searching for these we discovered Roman remains, the existence of which no one suspected. This proved that there had been a Roman settlement at Baginton and so we kept a vigilant watch and have since been able to prove the existence of a Romano-British settlement covering quite a long period. In addition we have found remains of the Bronze Age.

The Roman remains were found in a gravel pit within sight of the famous Baginton Oak. In this pit Mr Edwards found a small piece of Roman pottery and subsequent digging unearthed a well in which was found a large amount of pottery, a skull, a 1st-century brooch and coin of Nero, and objects associated with women and children. From this time on Baginton was thought to have had a Roman villa or farmstead.

Baginton Corn Mill as it was in 1918.

This belief persisted into the 1950s, until subsequent excavations proved otherwise and Baginton was found to have been the site of a large Roman legionary fort, the only one in Western Europe to have a '*gyrus*' or ring, for battle conditioning horses. The fort appears to have been occupied in various stages from AD 60 to AD 260. The large numbers of horse-associated objects suggest the fort was at some point occupied by Roman cavalry legions. Interestingly there appears to have been intensive occupation in AD 60, the year of Boudica's devastating rebellion. Many of the horses captured after her defeat at Mancetter are believed to have been brought back to the site for conditioning in the *gyrus*. Between 1970 and 1973 parts of the fort were reconstructed using the original techniques in the original postholes. These included the east gate, rebuilt by the Royal Engineers, and the Granary. The result was the Lunt Roman Fort, a popular destination for tourists and school parties.

As the gravel workings expanded behind the old post office and the row of cottages which back onto the airport, another surprise discovery came to light: an Anglo-Saxon pagan cemetery. Around 100 cremation burials were unearthed. Buried in urns, the remains of men were accompanied by objects to take into the afterlife such as swords, spears, shields and buckets, which may have originally contained food. The burials of women were accompanied by jewellery, such as brooches and amber beads from the Baltic.

One large decorative bronze bowl which was used as a cremation bowl became known as the 'Baginton Bowl' and is one of the best examples to survive from the late 5th to early 6th century. It is believed to be Celtic rather than Saxon.

Mr J. Edwards, the man who discovered the first Roman remains, also started excavating another of the village's historical sites, Baginton Castle, which overlooked the River Sowe. The castle appears to date from the late 14th century and was probably built by Sir William Bagot on the site of an older unidentified building belonging to Sir Richard Herthill.

William Bagot was no ordinary local lord but a member of King Richard II's Privy Council and one of the king's closest advisors. He was described by Walsingham as 'avaricious, ambitious and arrogant.' He led the prosecution of those who opposed Richard II. He is also noted for having once attacked the walls of Coventry.

Bagot also gave lodging to Henry Bolingbroke (later Henry IV), Duke of Hereford, in September 1398 before the combat on Gosford Green with Thomas Mowbray, Duke of Norfolk. The *Holinshed Chronicle* records that 'The sundaie before the fight, after dinner, the duke of Hereford came to the king (being lodged about a quarter of a mile without the towne in a tower that belonged to Sir William Bagot) to take his leave of him.' Bolingbroke rode from Baginton Castle 'mounted on a white courser, barded with green and blue velvet and embroided sumptuously with swans and antelopes.' Before the combat took place both men were exiled and Bolingbroke later returned and took the throne from Richard.

As Henry IV Bolingbroke executed Bagot's fellow lords and Bagot himself fled to Ireland before being taken and imprisoned in the Tower of London. He died in 1407 and in Baginton church there is a fine memorial brass of William and his wife.

The castle and the manor were acquired by Richard Beauchamp, Earl of Warwick and patron to the young Henry VI. Around this time the castle was probably demolished as Richard already had nearby Warwick Castle and the remaining manor was conveyed to the Collegiate Church of St Mary in Warwick in 1471. In 1544 it came into the hands of the Goodere family. The most famous of them was Sir Henry Goodere, who also had a home in Much Park Street, Coventry, and at Polesworth. Sir Henry's page was Warwickshire's second most notable poet John Drayton, who during his time with Sir Henry fell in love with his daughter, Anne.

Baginton Fields Farm in 1918.

Sir Henry also had a soft spot for Mary Queen of Scots, and during her imprisonment in Coventry he often visited her and is believed to have carried messages for her. For this the Queen rewarded him with a set of gold studs. The other Queen, Elizabeth, sent him to the Tower, although he later regained royal favour.

In 1618 the estate was sold to Sir William Bromley, who built a new house near the centre of the village. Sir William was a staunch Royalist during the Civil War and his tombstone in the church bears these words: 'He did not degenerate from his renowned ancestors, firmly adhering to King Charles, the Blessed Martyr, and taken fighting for him. He shared in the common calamity, sequestration and imprisonment. At last he was obliged, till the happy Restoration delivered him, not to go above two miles, from home without leave.'

His son, who inherited the estate, was also called Sir William; he was an MP and Speaker of the House of Commons and also Secretary of State in the reign of Queen Anne. He also had secret allegiances to the Jacobites.

This William probably enlarged or refaced the hall and made a beautiful residence set in formal gardens. In 1706, however, 'a dreadful fire consumed the Manor House and furniture, a large library of books and manuscripts, with most of the writings belonging to the family.' Despite this disaster Sir William rebuilt in a similar style, the house described as 'an elegant pile of a building.' Over the entrance was the family motto, 'Du Patru Servate Domum, 1714.'

Sir William died in 1732 and his heir died five years later. The last in line of the Bromley family was a lady said to have died in 1822. The estate then came to the Davenports, who were related to the Bromleys by marriage. The Revd Walter Davenport became the owner and from 1850 to 1858 the hall was leased to the Right Hon William Yates Peel, younger brother of the famous Robert Peel, Prime Minister and founder of the metropolitan police.

The estate was then inherited by the son of the Revd Walter Davenport Bromley, who changed his name by deed poll to Bromley Davenport. During his ownership, under the tenancy of Mr W.S. Armitage, the house was again destroyed by fire. On 7 October 1889 the butler refilled an oil lamp, which he lit. For some reason it exploded in flames, starting a fire which quickly got out of control.

A mounted messenger was sent to Coventry and the Coventry Fire Brigade rushed to Baginton with their horse-drawn steam-powered appliance. A press report stated that crowds of people followed, including a detachment of about 30 men of the Royal Field Artillery who were based in the barracks. They helped to clear the rooms of the hall. Initially there were problems piping the water but this was quickly solved with the arrival of more pipes. A single stream of water was played onto the burning building and dozens of people resorted to the bucket. Captain Thomas, Lieutenant Smith and Private Stratham of the fire service, together with an artillery sergeant, were fighting the fire in the Gun Room when there was a huge explosion and a plate glass door shattered, injuring them all.

Soon more fire appliances arrived but the fire took six hours to bring under control and the hall was lost. The burnt-out building stood forlorn amid an overgrown estate until it was sold by auction in 1918 and came under the control of the Coventry Corporation. Later the estate was sold to a builder from Leamington, who restored the wings of the hall and rented them out in 1926.

The estate then came into the hands of Edward Bowden, who built many of the houses in the village. He also created an Assembly Hall in the hall, which was used by the villagers, along with the grounds, with Mr Bowden's blessing. Bowden planned to turn the hall into an auditorium and factory but his plans never reached fruition. The shell of the hall stood for many years until it was finally demolished. There is little now to suggest it ever existed at all. In around 1927 the Russell brothers, Jack and Reg, acquired eight acres by Baginton Bridge to produce plants for sale in Coventry. Since those early days Coventry's oldest established plant nursery has grown, as has its reputation.

Another building that stood near the castle site was a solid square stone structure surmounted by a tiled roof. No one appears to know what it was although many stories were told of it. One claims that one of the hall's owners offended the reigning monarch and, instead of being beheaded, was incarcerated in this building and had his property confiscated.

Another story says that a knight who lived here left his home and wife in the capable hands of his squire. On his return he found he had been betrayed and the squire was imprisoned in the building, languishing there until he died. The final story dates from more recent times and claims that the building was used for quoit players. During a game one of the players is said to have thrown his quoit so hard that it overshot and rolled down the bank towards the river. The player pursued it, lost his footing and broke his neck and now haunts the spot.

The village's other important building is the fine 13th-century church of St John the Baptist, which was once a chapelry served by Kenilworth Priory. The church has an unusual wooden bell turret and inside retains its box pews and royal coat of arms. The former Lady Chapel contains many memorials in stone and glass to the Bromley family and on the south wall of the chancel is the fine

The Lunt Cottages, Baginton, some of which still stand next to the Lunt Roman fort.

brass to Sir William Bagot and Margaret his wife. Outside in the churchyard can be seen memorials to other owners and tenants of the hall, along with the graves of a number of airmen, fighter pilots who flew from the nearby airfield during World War Two.

The site of the airfield at Baginton was purchased in 1935, near the Whitley works of Armstrong Whitworth Aircraft. AWA, as it was known, wanted a larger airfield, as did Coventry City Council, which welcomed the prospect of establishing the city's own airfield. AWA built a new factory next to the airfield and in May 1936 moved production of the Whitley bomber there.

All the Whitleys up to the Mark VII were built in Baginton and they formed the backbone of the RAF during the early days of World War Two. Bombers from here (and the Whitley factory) were the first to penetrate German airspace, but despite proving their worth they are now almost forgotten.

In the autumn of 1940 fighter squadron No.9 was based at the airfield, and the Oak (opened 1926) was used as their base. On 25 September 1940 a Polish squadron flying Hurricanes, No.308, was based here, surprising locals as they dressed in riding breeches. Because most raids in the area took place at night their effectiveness was limited. The squadron did however force a Junker 88 to dump its load after an unsuccessful attempt to bomb the AWA factory.

In March 1941 a squadron of Tomahawks were also based at the site and in April 308 Squadron was re-equipped with Spitfires. Both squadrons left Baginton and were replaced by 605 Squadron, which was joined in June 1941 by 457 Squadron. In August 1941 Baginton ceased to be a Sector Station and the fighters pulled out. Thereafter it was a kitting-out station for fighter squadrons.

Between March 1937 and June 1943 AWA built 1,812 Whitley bombers, but none survive. The firm also built Albemarles, Manchesters, Lincolns, Wellingtons and the famous Lancaster bomber. The Meteor jet fighter was built there in 1944, carrying jet engines developed by Coventry kid Sir Frank Whittle. The factory also built the futuristic AW52 Flying Wing, an aircraft that was 50 years ahead of its time and was tested over Baginton. AWA continued production of transporters like the Argosy, fighters such as the Meteor WS838, and missiles such as the Sea Slug until its closure in 1965.

Baginton Airport flew its first civilian flights in 1952 and created its first hard runway. From this time it staged regular air shows and became one of the country's top venues. In 1998 the Atlantique Group took control of the airport, which now deals mainly with air freight. Baginton's flying past is well represented by the Midland Air Museum, which was started in 1967 by a small group of enthusiasts. Today the self-funding enterprise has on show a large number of aircraft and includes the Sir Frank Whittle Jet Heritage Centre, which displays, among other things, one of his early jet engines.

One of Baginton's claims to fame is its connection to the novelist George Eliot (Mary Ann Evans), who visited her aunt, Fanny Houghton, who lived in the village. During those visits she met and fell in love with a young man, a picture restorer. After two days in his company Mary Ann told her friends that he was the most interesting young man she had ever met and superior to the rest of mankind. However, after he proposed Mary Ann turned him down, despite much heartache, because his profession was unsuitable. The name of Mary Ann's first love is not recorded, but some have suggested that he worked at the hall, although he could have also been a resident of Baginton.

Before we leave Baginton let's not forget the famous Baginton Oak, which when it was last measured in 1932 had a girth at the base of some 40ft. It has grown since but only slowly. The oak is probably about 500 years old, so its leaves were waving in the breeze when Shakespeare was but a lad.

The tree has many stories associated with it including the fact that it was once used by a witches' coven, although as it stands on the fork of two roads this hardly seems likely. Another story tells of a traveller taking refuge in the tree many centuries ago when he was being pursued by wolves. The tree saved his life and in gratitude he left money to the village known as the 'Wolf Charity.' In the 1930s the tree had huge splits in its trunk, which were surprisingly filled with concrete. Thankfully there are no more wild wolves roaming Baginton but the Baginton Oak still stands, one of Warwickshire's greatest living trees.

Further Reading
Baginton after the Bromleys: The Village in the 20th Century, Baginton History Group, 1995.
Miscellaneous news cuttings in Local Studies.

BINLEY

Binley was called Bilnei in the Domesday Book of 1086, and is believed to mean 'Billa's well-watered land.' Ernsford comes from the, 'Eagle's ford,' or the 'ford of a man called Ern.'

In the Domesday Book Binley is recorded as being in the Stoneleigh Hundred held partly by St Mary's, Coventry. It states there were three hides (a hide was enough land to support a household) and eight ploughs. In the demesne (the lord's home-farm) was one plough with four slaves and ten villeins (a peasant of high status) and six boarders (cottagers or peasants of low status) with two ploughs and one slave. There were also woods half a mile long. The survey records that in Saxon times Ealdgyth, wife of Gruffydd, held the land before the Conquest, when it was passed to Osbern FitzRichard who sold it to the prior of Coventry.

The rest of the village was at that time held by Eadwulf as a tenant of Thorkil, Earl of Warwick. This consisted of two hides of land in which there were six ploughs, five villeins, seven boarders and two slaves. There was also a mill valued at 40d, meadows and woodland.

Dugdale records that Thurbert, son of Hadulfus (Eadwulf) gave the monks of Coombe a large portion of the estate, upon which it is said that he and his wife, 'betook themselves to a retired life in that monastery, the monks giving them allowance of diet during their lives; also Henry his son and heir, two marks of silver; and the rest of the children 12d, apiece.'

At about the same time Ralph de Bilneje also gave the monks a large amount of land, whereupon 'he had allowance of his diet as long as he lived.' This daily allowance, which was the same as a monk's, was also given to his mother. His brother, on confirmation of this, received a horse, two marks and

The old Binley Bridge, photographed in around 1912. (CCL)

Abbey Cottages in Willenhall Lane, photographed in 1925 and built as part of the Binley miners' village.(CCL)

four shillings in silver. Robert's son also gave the monks woodland at Binley on condition that on his death the monks would give him an appropriate send off, hopefully into heaven.

It is said that by 1279 the monks of Coombe had at Binley one caracute (enough to be ploughed by an eight-ox team) of land, a water mill, two windmills, five cottages, and 42 acres of woodland, two of them in Brandon Park. The monks of Coombe also held rights to hold court here and had a gallows and the assize of bread and beer. After the Dissolution of the Monasteries the abbey became Crown property until it passed to John Dudley, Earl of Warwick, and then to Robert Kelway, who sold it to John Harington of Exton.

Within Binley stood two granges, working farms belonging to Coombe, Binley Grange and Ernsford Grange. Binley Grange was built on land given by Thurbat, son of Eadwulf, to the abbot of Coombe in the 12th century. The grange, with a windmill, was standing in 1291 and later became Binley Grange Farm.

The Adam-style St Bartholomew's Church off the Brinklow Road. (CCL)

Ernsford Grange was originally a small hamlet called Ernsford inhabited by about six families in around 1280. The land was given as a gift to Coombe and afterwards Ernsford Grange was built, probably as a farm dealing with Coombe's enormous flock of sheep. After the Dissolution under Henry VIII the grange came into the hands of Thomas Brooke and John Williams in 1544, then passed to Charles Waryn and his heirs. The grange was excavated in 1972 during the building of Ernsford Grange Comprehensive School and the base of a substantial L-shaped stone building, built in two periods, was unearthed. The building evidently had leaded windows, tiled floors and consisted of a kitchen, hall, chamber and garderobe. In the silt of the garderobe were found a green-glazed pot-bellied jug and a large bowl, both almost complete. The floor of the garderobe was a puzzle, as it was made of large slabs of chalk not

Binley Colliery, photographed in around 1925, before the Great Strike. (CCL)

The junction of the Binley, Brandon and Brinklow roads in around 1920. The cottages on the right are now gone and the unenclosed area in the foreground was the meeting place of the Warwickshire Hunt when Dan Claridge ran the Craven Arms behind. (CCL)

available locally. A building still stood here in the 18th century, for Henry Beighton's map of 1722 records a grange here. Up until the early 1960s a farmhouse and outbuildings called Ernesford Grange stood adjacent to the northern side of the moat and the area enclosed by the moat was an orchard. The dried-up moat of the original grange can still be seen at the entrance to the school.

The original church dedicated to St Swithin was built probably as a chapel of ease in the 12th century by John de Peyto. Tradition says that previously the inhabitants had to go to Stoke to receive the sacrament, but one would assume that in those early days if the river was forded it would sometimes flood, making it impossible to reach the church, hence the need for a chapel of ease. The chapel was soon after granted to Coventry Priory by the Earl of Chester. After the Dissolution it fell into private hands and later, along with Coombe, passed to the Cravens. This church, considered dark and ancient, was pulled down in 1771 and a new church, built in the latest Adam style and dedicated

The original Binley Toll Gate cottage on the Binley Road. It actually stood in the parish of Stoke near the junction of the present Hipswell Highway.

to St Bartholomew, was erected at the expense of the Earl of Craven.

Binley Mill was first mentioned in 1068 as being held by Eadwulf from Thorkil and worth 40d. The watermill that stood here until the 1960s was believed to have been built in 1813. When the mill came up for sale in 1923 as part of the Coombe Abbey estate it was described as Binley Mill Farm, consisting of a cottage, mill-house, farm buildings, orchard, millstream and pond. The mill farm and 55 acres of land were then let to Mr H. Skelton for £124 per year. The race and dam were filled in during the 1950s when the mill wheel was removed. The site of the mill now houses coaches of Coventry's most noted coaching company, Harry Shaw.

Another building up for sale in 1923 was the Craven Arms Hotel. This 18th-century inn stood on the site of Binley gallows, the place of execution of Sir Henry Mumford and Sir Robert Mallory for treason in 1495. The two lords were beheaded here and afterwards their heads decorated two of the city gates. On this corner also stood the Maiden's Cross, a stone late-mediaeval cross. During the

Building a new bridge on the Binley Road in 1912. This ancient boundary point was where important visitors to Coventry were met. (CCL)

18th century the inn was the meeting place for a 'thief-taking society', which offered rewards for the conviction of criminals. From the late 19th century the landlord was the noted Dan Claridge, the last man to drive a stagecoach to London. Dan, who died in 1923, could often be seen with his white side whiskers, dressed in a frock coat and top hat, welcoming the Atherstone Hunt which used to gathered at the inn.

Another noted Binley-born character was the Revd Thomas Wagstaffe, who wrote a defence of King Charles I. Wagstaffe lived in France for many years as the chaplain to the Jacobite Pretender, Charles Stewart, and his son, Bonnie Prince Charlie. He died there in 1770.

Interestingly in 1924 the *Coventry Standard* thought that many must be

The interior of the Craven's Binley Church in the late 1940s. The family crest can be seen behind the light bearing the motto, 'Virtus consistit in actione.'

The junction of Brinklow Road and Clifford Bridge Road in around 1925. One of these thatched cottages survived to become Lino's restaurant.

The Craven Arms in the early 1930s. An inn by that name has stood on this old gallows site since the 18th century.

'struck by the numerous signs of development' taking place in Binley. In 1904 there were no more than 40 houses in the village and by 1911 this had increased by only five. However, by 1924 the number had increased to 162, with 835 inhabitants. The main reason for the expansion of the village was Binley Colliery.

Work began on sinking a shaft in May 1907 and by the end of 1908 the coal seam had been reached. In 1924 500 men worked the colliery, including many Scots who had formed the original workforce. To house these men estates were built around Willenhall Lane, Binley Avenue, Coombe Avenue, Craigends Avenue and Grange Avenue. This became known as 'Binley Village' and the rural community was gradually taken over by miners from all over Britain and abroad. The pit continued to maintain much of the community until its closure in 1963, when the village, overlooked by a mountainous spoil heap, had a population of 3,028, the majority of whom were dependant upon the colliery.

Much of the impetus to expand the village came from the sale of the Coombe Abbey estate in 1923. While much of the village was under the Cravens of Coombe little

An 1848 engraving of the noted Binley Oak, which in 1888 measured 32ft around the base, 18ft 5in around the middle and 65ft high. This now gone great oak stood off the Brinklow Road near the present Hunters Close.

development had occurred, but the sale of the estate land opened up the area for development. John McKinley purchased Ernesford Grange Farm and farmed the land, but sold a small acreage to a Welsh builder called Howarth who wanted to create a Welsh village. He built several houses of a unique style in Brookvale Avenue but failed to complete it before the great strike of 1926 ruined his business.

When World War Two ended Newcombe Estates acquired land bordered by Binley Road, colliery houses and the railway line. This was built upon and became the Ernesford Grange Estate. Other builders bought in and development began on what became Ullswater Road. Residents moved into the development on George Marston Road in 1956 and work began on houses on the Binley Road in 1957. Early in 1964 work began on housing joining Willenhall Lane and this was later continued by council-funded building, which in 1970 included flats. By this time the population of the once rural village had leapt to 13,800.

Binley Woods was originally a thickly wooded area, which began to be encroached upon in the 1920s after the sale of the Coombe Abbey estate. By the 1930s a scattering of houses lay along the Rugby Road and during the war others moved here. Bombed out of the city or seeking safety they lived in caravans and temporary huts. By the late 1950s a distinct community had built up, which chose to call the area Binley Woods. Among the area's most noted residents are the 'Coventry Bees', whose track at their stadium has been the home of Coventry speedway for many years.

Further Reading
Sir William Dugdale, *Warwickshire*, 1817, revised.
Binley & its Heritage, sponsored by Harry Shaw Travel.
Newspapers in Local Studies.
R.J. Carter, *A History of Binley*, 1973.

THE BUTTS

The Butts was originally called the Summerland Butts and it was somewhere here in mediaeval times that Coventrians practiced their archery as directed by law. The Leet Book of 1468 states, 'It is ordained that the Butts about this city be made and that no-man within this city from henceforth shoot at rovers, but at butts and standing targets.' This area was outside the city wall and it was not until the 19th century that buildings first began to be erected. These areas were known as the Poddy Croft, the Six Closes and the Bull Fields, now the Butts. Within the area lay Crow Moat, the only moated house to lie within a short distance of the old city wall.

In 1820 Hertford Terrace, Hertford Square and Junction Street were built on a piece of land called Barber's Close and in 1832 around Crow Moat were built Thomas Street, Moat Street and Albion Street. Parochially the district was in the parish of St John's but it was reassigned to its own district of St Thomas's.

A piece of land was acquired for £81 from the freemen to build the church dedicated to St Thomas. Some were not happy with this arrangement as when the church was being erected in 1848 the masons received threats that what they put up in the day would be taken down at night. Despite this the church, built with stone given by Lord Leigh from a quarry off the Kenilworth Road, was eventually completed and the first vicar appointed by Sir Robert Peel was the Revd Stephen Cragg, who continued there until 1883.

A cycle race taking place at the Butts track in 1948.

The Butts Technical College in The Butts, photographed in the 1940s.

The Vignoles bridge, photographed in a relandscaped Butts in the kate 1960s.

A Fred Taunton engraving of St Thomas's Church in The Butts as it appeared in 1865.

Times were often difficult. In 1868 the yearly collection only amounted to £29 and soon after the choir went on strike. In 1875 no one would stand as church or parish warden. In 1890 the church was so far behind with its bills that it had to go back to candle power as the gas company cut off its supply. The church thrived in the 20th century but in 1972 it was estimated that £150,000 was needed to restore the building and it was decided to close it. Parishioners fought back and the church was listed as a building of special interest. This was, however, only a local listing and in 1975 the church that some didn't want built was finally demolished.

The Butts, like Spon Street, Spon End, Chapelfields and Earlsdon, was originally an extension to the watch-making district spilling out of Spon Street. Makers were still there in the late 19th century such as Issac Jebez Theo Newsome at numbers 14 and 15 and Charles Read at 13 Hope Street, Summerland Place.

Coventry Technical College was built in 1935 on a former cricket ground and behind it stood the Butt Stadium, opened in 1879 as a cycle track and testing place for some of the country's earliest motorcycles.

Further Reading
Newspapers, Local Studies.

CALUDON

The name of Caludon comes from '*callod*' and '*don*', meaning mossy rise. The area is most famous for its castle, but the first mention of the manor comes in around 1200 when Ranulf Blundeville, Earl of Chester, gave it to Stephen de Segrave, who had accompanied him on a trip to the Holy Land. Segrave was given the estate and whatever building stood on it, for a peppercorn rent of one sparrowhawk a year. Historical sources tell us that Stephen died in 1241, leaving a manor house here with a chapel in its grounds. There may have also been 20 acres of parkland and a pool at this time, although this is not mentioned until 1279. Stephen's heir John de Segrave obtained permission from Edward I in 1305 to fortify the manor house of Caludon and surround it with a moat.

When John died in 1353 the manor passed, through his daughter Elizabeth, to her husband John Mowbray. In 1354 Mowbray was granted further licences to rebuild and extend the fortified manor house. It was during this period that Caludon manor house became Caludon Castle. John and Elizabeth's son, Thomas Mowbray, Duke of Norfolk, was accused by Henry Bolingbroke of treasonable words against Richard II. Thomas stayed at Caludon the night before his trial by combat against Bolingbroke on Gosford Green. As the men faced each other the combat was halted and after two hours of discussion the king banished both men from the realm. Thomas Mowbray never returned, but Bolingbroke later deposed the king and was crowned Henry IV. He ordered the execution of Mowbray's heir and Caludon began to fall into ruins.

In 1491 William, Lord Berkeley, acquired the castle, which remained in the family until 1631. It is said that the family rebuilt the castle in around 1530. In 1536 Isabel Berkeley, wife of Lord Maurice Berkeley, died at the castle aged 70. Her funeral was quite extraordinary. She ordered that the Psalms of David be read continually until she was interred. Groups of priests stood over her, continually praying from Wednesday till Monday. She paid for all the church bells of Coventry to be rung continually. Her funeral cortège left Caludon at night, led by 30 women carrying tall candles wearing black gowns and with kerchiefs on their heads. They were followed by 33 crafts guilds bearing 200 torches, then 30 of her own servants, dressed in black and carrying torches. Next came monks from the Greyfriars and Whitefriars carrying crosses, followed by over 100 priests with crosses and the hearse, trailed by 'gentlewomen mourners', the mayor of Coventry, masters of the guilds and the aldermen, sheriffs, chamberlains and wardens.

Lady Isabel's body was taken to Coventry Priory and there, surrounded by hundreds of candles, was laid in state in the choir before the high altar where dirges were sung. On Monday the same cavalcade took her down the Binley Road to Binley Bridge where they were met by the Lord Abbot of Coombe Abbey. Here it is said 5–6,000 people sat down at tables to eat before moving on to Coombe where she was buried.

Caludon passed to Maurice, 4th Lord Berkeley, who let the building to a relative, Thomas Try. The manor then passed to Lord Thomas who passed it on through Lady Ann Berkeley, who had once been maid of honour to Anne Boleyn. Meanwhile the life tenant Thomas Try died and Lady Ann, despite

The only surviving fragment of Caludon Castle, the end of the great banqueting hall, photographed in the 1940s.

the lease and the presence of his son and wife at the castle, tried to take possession. Two years later a bill of Chancery came out in her favour and she moved in.

After his mother's death in 1564 Lord Henry Berkeley took up residence at the castle. Henry and his wife, Lady Katherine, the daughter of the Duke of Norfolk, lived in style, and their household numbered some 70 persons. It is recorded in 1580 that Lord Henry had the roofs of the old castle buildings taken off and so altered that it looked like a different building. He also built a porter's lodge and other buildings inside the moat, as well as adding buildings outside, including a new brew house and stables.

Also in 1580 it is recorded in *Lives of the Berkeleys* that Lady Katherine, known as a haughty individual, was in contact with a noted wizard known locally as 'Old Bourne.' Her servant opened one of her letters to the wizard, read it and kept it and when it was discovered that he was fiddling building expenses for the gatehouse he tried to blackmail the lady with it. Lady Berkeley had the letter stolen back and burned and the servant dismissed before her name got too involved with witchcraft.

A watercolour by C. Varley of Caludon Castle as it appeared in around 1800.

Lord Henry, unlike his wife, was loved by all. He was charitable and always carried money to give to the poor. Three days a week pottage, bread, beef, mutton and beer were distributed to the local poor from his gate. At Christmas when he feasted in the great banqueting hall he would leave his seat at the top of the table and individually greet all his guests. If he had a guest of importance he always gave them his own seat at the top of the table and went and sat among the meaner company at the lower end.

The building is believed to have been added to by Elizabeth Berkeley in the 17th century. During the Civil War it was probably besieged by Parliamentarian forces, who camped in a field between Stoke Aldermoor and Henley Mill called Camp Field. The *Coventry Standard* of 1926 records a tradition among the inhabitants of this district of a battle taking place, which may be a folk memory of the siege of Caludon. In 1926 a V-shaped trench existed running from the spring to the higher ground towards the end of Wyken Lane (now Blackberry Lane). Local tradition holds that the soldiers used this during the siege of the castle.

The castle was left in ruins and the three-acre Great Pool was drained. In the late 18th century it was acquired by the Cliffords (Clifford Bridge) who built a large farmhouse from the remains of Caludon. This building survived into the 20th century. It appears that until the 19th century the castle remains were fairly extensive, including a tower with battlements. What has survived into the 20th and 21st century is basically the seven-foot thick wall of the banqueting hall. This was likely to have been built by John, Lord Mowbray, under his licence of 1354.

Near the ruins lie the remains of a number of other moats, one of which may belong to an earlier form of the building. The field to the south of the ruin was always known as the Park, and on the brow of the hill there is another moated area measuring some 60 square yards. On the south side the remains of a defensive structure or rampart existed until the 1920s. The raised area known as the

Bowling Green is of unknown date but Roman pottery has been found there. It seems possible that the site was inhabited in Roman times, since some sort of Roman building, perhaps a farm or small villa, once stood at Mount Pleasant in nearby Walsgrave.

During the 14th century when England was at war with France and English armies did not wish to fly the banner of saintly Edward the Confessor it was decided to promote the warrior Saint George to national saint. A new legend was created to make George an Englishman, and his birthplace was given as Caludon Castle.

The legend runs that in the distant past Lord Albert, High Steward of England, and his wife lived at Caludon. Albert's wife was pregnant and having strange dreams so he went to a local grove to consult the enchantress Kalyb. He was informed that his wife would die giving birth to a special son, a champion of England, who would bear a birthmark – the mark of the dragon.

Albert returned to Caludon to find the boy born and his wife dead. During the night while he and the castle mourned Kalyb entered the castle and stole the baby. Albert searched the land in vain before travelling abroad and dying on a fruitless quest to find his son. Meanwhile the baby grew into a boy, then a man, trained by Kalyb, who butchered babies and kept their remains in a cave.

When he reached the age of 21 George, now great in arms, wished to leave the witch but Kalyb contrived to make him stay. First she took him to a golden castle in which she had by magic imprisoned the Six Champions of Christendom. She told him if he stayed he could become the seventh. George could not be tempted. She then showed him several white horses and offered him Bayard, the swiftest of them all. George refused. She gave him invincible armour and the magic sword Ascalon, but George still refused to stay.

Lastly in desperation Kalyb offered him her own magic wand. George took it and struck it against a rock, exposing the cave where Kalyb kept the remains of her child victims. He pushed her in and the cave sealed up forever. George then took all Kalyb had offered him and rode off and released the Champions, bringing them back to Coventry. Here they stayed for nine months honing their skills in combat before riding off south and to various adventures abroad.

St George went to Egypt, fought a dragon and won the heart of the Princess Sabra, had more adventures, became ruler of the east and finally returned home with the princess. There is a verse from Bishop Percy's *Reliques of Ancient English Poetry* which reads:

> Wherein with his dear love he lived,
> And fortune did their nuptials grace;
> They many years of joy did see
> And lived their lives at Coventree.

Further Reading

David McGrory, *Coventry: The Making of a City*, *Coventry Evening Telegraph* supplements.

E. Hodges, *The Old Homes of the Berkeleys*, *Coventry Standard*, 1894.

Caludon Castle: Its History & Traditions.

News cuttings, Local studies.

CANLEY

The name Canley comes from the Anglo-Saxon, and means 'Canna's clearing.' A Neolithic stone axe called the Canley Axe was discovered in the late 1940s on land off Kirby Corner. Its importance, apart from showing early occupation or passage through the area, was that it was of a scarce type known as a Graig Llwyd axe. Produced at a prehistoric axe factory in Wales it is one of only three such axes found in Coventry (the others were from Baginton and Gibbet Hill). Considering that the number of such axes found in England is very small the finding of three of these Welsh axes in such a small area is very significant and suggests that this part of Coventry may lie on an ancient prehistoric trade route from the Menai Straits.

Canley originally belonged to the Crown and in 1154 it was acquired by Cistercian monks who set up their abbey at Stoneleigh. It appears that during the 13th century Ketelbern de Canley, a wealthy freeman, began paying his neighbours' rents and over the following years took control of the lordship. In 1266 his son Robert de Canley was claiming the title of lord of the manor. The monks of Stoneleigh, the real lords, brought an action against him and recovered the lordship. It is recorded that the documents of possession were delivered to the abbot of Stoneleigh by command of the King at Stoneleigh Cross and Robert de Canley was stripped of his acquisitions and only allowed by the abbot's grace to keep his family's original two yardland. After the Dissolution in 1539 Canley was passed onto the Duke of Suffolk and some years later part of it was sold to Sir Thomas Leigh, then Lord Mayor of London. By 1800 the Leighs of Stoneleigh had amassed over 20,000 acres of land, which formed the Stoneleigh Estate. This included Canley, Fletchamstead and Westwood Heath. The land remained the property of the Leighs until 1926 when it was sold to Coventry Corporation. It did not become part of Coventry until it was added to the county borough in 1930.

Canley's most famous resident was Henry Parkes, the 'Father of the Federation', who was born at Moat House Cottage, tucked behind the fire station off Fletchamstead Highway. Parkes was born in 1815, the youngest son of a tenant farmer, in the timbered building in what was then part of Moat House Lane. He was baptised at Stoneleigh church, then the parish church, and was educated at Stoneleigh School until the age of 11.

When the family fell on hard times they moved to Birmingham and Henry was apprenticed into the ivory turning trade. He married a Kenilworth girl and moved to

Looking down the Kenilworth Road towards Coventry in around 1910. On the left is Gibbet Hill Road and on the right, off the picture, is the Stoneleigh Road. Just below this point stood the gibbet from which the hill takes its name. (CCL)

Canley waterfall by Canley Ford in around 1905, a popular destination for many locals. Kingfishers can be seen there. (CCL)

London, but after his business collapsed and his two children died Henry and his wife Clarinda decided to start afresh in 1839 by emigrating to Australia, where he set up a fancy goods shop in Sydney.

Henry got involved in politics and started to campaign to end the transportation of convicts to the colony. By 1850 he was the leader of the movement and started a weekly newspaper called *The Empire*. In 1854 he was elected to the New South Wales Parliament. Henry Parkes fought to improve hospitals, prisons and the lives of small farmers. He became Prime Minister in 1878, the first of five times and was knighted by Queen Victoria in 1882. By the end of the decade his work had led to the establishment of the Commonwealth of Australia. The Canley boy who united Australia, Sir Henry Parkes died aged 81 on 30 April 1896.

The 200-year-old Moat House Cottage (previously called Moat House) came into the hands of the city council when it purchased land off the Stoneleigh Estate in 1926, including Tile Hill, Canley and Westwood. It is a Grade II listed building much visited by Australian tourists. Nearby lies the site of an older moat; this may have some connection to the long-gone Morhalle Manor.

Another famous name associated with the area is the noted novelist E.M. Forster, writer of such novels as *A Room with a View*. Forster died while staying with his friends Mr and Mrs Bob Buckingham in Salisbury Avenue in Stivichall. His ashes were scattered at Canley Crematorium (opened 1943) off Charter Avenue.

The original tiny village of Canley consisted of a small number of cottages, which lay scattered below Ivy Farm, based around the present Ivy Farm Lane, Cannock's Lane and Cannon Hill Road. Cannon Hill Road, previously unnamed, led up Watery Lane and across Canley Ford, with its waterfall, a favourite day trip for Coventrians. Apart from an odd house much of the district was farmland noted for its oaks and deep lanes.

The Moat House, birthplace of Sir Henry Parkes, still visited today by Australian tourists. (CCL)

In 1937 historian Mary Dormer Harris wrote:

> *At Canley, one misses at once the ford, where our old grey horse used to stop and drink. The little stone bridge is ship-shape . . . only forgive me for saying I liked better the old wooden footbridge and the sight of the running stream. You see I was familiar with it all, many years ago. Canley is transmogrified too, evidently in train for a new suburb, the lanes indicated by miniature signposts, waiting to be turned into real streets. There are villas in the lane towards Fletchamstead gate, and allotments with yellow flowering cabbages come up close to the house itself.*

In the *Coventry Standard* in 1960, reporter Brian Devine wrote of the district:

> *In the last 40 or 50 years a lot has happened in Canley which has changed its character completely. Years ago the whole area was divided up into two farms, Silk's and Capel's. Down on the outside fringe of the development area, a small path still runs down to the railway crossing keeper's house, close by the railway. For the past 30 years Mr and Mrs Frank Heathfield have lived there — Mrs Heathfield is still employed as the crossing keeper.*
>
> *Years ago the crossing was built to let cattle and vehicles going to Silk's Farm cross the lines. This is all that remains of the farm community whose lands stretched as far as one could see from the old cottage windows. A little farther away, four old gnarled trees is all that is left of a little row of farm workers' cottages and gardens that were occupied when the farms were working fully.*
>
> *From the cottage garden the landscape to the left is covered by the high flats and houses of Tile Hill. Across to the front, the Canley development stretches away to the main road. Mr Heathfield, who has seen this gradual transformation over the years, did not appear to have any regrets, 'When I first came here it was very beautiful all around here. I met and married my wife, who was a servant girl at Silk's,' he said pointing over to a clump of fir trees where the farm once stood.*

A drawing by Coventry benefactor and mayor John Gulson of a sunken lane somewhere in Canley in May 1849. (CCL)

Ancient survivals in the area are Park and Ten Shilling Wood in Charter Avenue, which are shown on the earliest map dating to 1776. These were once much larger mediaeval 'pasture woodland' in which pigs were grazed on acorns. During the Leighs' ownership the woodlands were coppiced and gun permits were issued for shooting pheasant and other game. A permit for Ten Shilling Wood was, unsurprisingly, 10 shillings, and the larger Park Wood, once known as Fifty Shilling Wood, cost 50 shillings.

Cannon Park, which is now better known for its shopping centre, has a copy of a 17th-century Civil War cannon outside one of its entrances. This is connected with a tradition that the site was used by Cromwell to store his cannon. Another version of the story tells that during the Civil War shots were fired on Coventry from here. Both stories are fanciful, but this part of the city does appear to have more than its fair share of Civil War tales. Perhaps an army garrison stopped here, using the back lanes to remain unseen, giving rise to the stories. Cannon Park may even have some older history, for many years ago a large amount of mediaeval pottery was found, which may be connected with a kiln in the area.

Gibbet Hill and the former Millburn Grange on the Kenilworth Road both lie within the parish boundary of Canley. Gibbet Hill was known as the Gallow hyll in 1546, so there is a history of executions on this high point. It takes its present name from an incident that took place in 1765. On Friday 16 March Thomas Edwards, a farmer, with John Green, a farm labourer, was in Coventry on market day. They met fellow farm worker John Spencer at the Hare & Squirrel in Coventry and as night fell they walked back home to Stoneleigh together.

Spencer and Green were fairly drunk but Edwards remained sober and carried a stout stick for protection. They crossed the fields and lanes before reaching the fields by Whoberley House. When they were 300 yards from the road Spencer and Green fell into an argument and Edwards walked ahead. Suddenly three men rushed out of the blackness and attacked them. Spencer and Green were beaten to the ground, but Edwards fought until he was bludgeoned with the metal butt of a pistol. The robbers took three half gold guineas and 11 shillings in silver.

After a short time Spencer and Green recovered and staggered off, not thinking to search for Edwards, who lay nearby in the darkness. Later he too regained his senses and struggled a quarter of a mile to the nearest house. He was taken in and put to bed in a serious condition. The following morning a boy found the pistol cock and a broken ramrod at the scene of the attack, which were taken

Canley Ford was a favourite spot in the 19th and 20th century. Here it is seen in the 1960s.

to Coventry to Alderman John Hewitt, three times mayor, justice and thief-taker. Hewitt recognised the parts as being from a military pistol and promptly contacted the regiment of dragoons who had been in the city. Enquiries and searches were made.

The following morning Hewitt was informed of Edwards's death. Hewitt wrote to Major Barber at Warwick with the names of the suspected murderers. When questioned Edward Drury turned King's Evidence against fellow soldier Robert Leslie and a third man to try to save his own neck. That night, with new evidence, Hewitt had a door beaten down in Spon Street, the home of Moses Baker, a weaver. The following day all three were together in Coventry Gaol. After some time the men confessed to the crime and were put on trial and found guilty.

The three men were sentenced to be hung and gibbeted on what was then Gallow Hill and on 17 April 1765 they were brought from Warwick in a open cart to a huge gallows. Before a crowd of thousands they were hung, taken down and tarred and rehung in a suit of chains. Forty-five years later the remains were taken down from Gibbet Hill and in 1822 it was reported that the gibbet still stood, leaning slightly because of the ghastly burden it had carried. During the latter part of the 19th century the gibbet was removed and some parts made into souvenirs such as rulers. The main part was taken to a local farm where it was used as a base for a hayrick. For years afterwards those who passed the spot hurried by for it was said on windy nights you could still hear the gibbet creaking and the chains rattling.

It is recorded that before the execution a local wise-woman predicted that if a hare started from under the gibbet a reprieve would be granted. Strangely this did happen, and a horseman was sent down the Kenilworth Road to check for a messenger bearing the reprieve. However, none was forthcoming and the execution went ahead.

Beyond Gibbet Hill past Wainbody Wood is the moat of Millburn Grange, called Melleburn in 1213. The grange belonged to the monks of Stoneleigh and it was from here in the reign of Elizabeth I that Lady Alice Leigh of Stoneleigh granted £29 per annum to be paid to the poor and for the maintenance of Stoneleigh church. This procedure was to be overseen by the mayor of Coventry.

Another grange in the area is Cryfield, the name said to come from the Anglo-Saxon meaning Crud's Field. Dugdale states that the kings of England had a house here before the Conquest. Tradition states that it was one of the residences of King Ethelred (978–1016). It is recorded that in the reign of Henry II (1154–1189) a foreign earl resided here by the King's leave. This earl was said to be a great robber who 'infested the country hereabouts very much.' The King eventually had him removed, although what he did is unrecorded.

Dugdale states that Henry II brought monks here from Radmore and depopulated the village, moving the inhabitants to Hurst, which no longer exists. Here he states they built a grange, which burned down due to the negligence of soldiers quartered there during the siege of Kenilworth Castle in 1266. In 1279 there was still a village here for it is recorded that they paid a stone of wax yearly for candles burning before the image of the Virgin in Stoneleigh Abbey. In 1284 Edward I granted the monks of Stoneleigh free warren (the sole right to exploit the game) of Cryfield, then referred to as Crulefield. The monks probably rebuilt the grange here at this time. The small hamlet was later depopulated again and by the late 15th century only the grange remained. The watermill, pool and meadows were leased out. After the Dissolution the grange came into the hands of Robert and Elizabeth Bocher. Robert was a servant in the royal court. Cryfield is now worked as a farm and has remnants of an older building at the rear. It also has a tradition attached to it, which states that there is a lost tunnel linking it to Kenilworth Castle.

The area between Gibbet Hill and Warwick University has for years yielded many prehistoric worked flint tools and arrowheads from the Neolithic to the Iron Age. In 1935 the Coventry Natural History and Scientific Society reported finding a green stone axe-head a short distance from Gibbet Hill. The axe was produced at the Graig Llwyd axe-factory in Wales and at the time was the first complete specimen to be found in England. From this rare find and others found in the area experts believe that Gibbet Hill lies on an ancient prehistoric trade route. In 2001–2, during work to lay a sports pitch at the university, one of the most important discoveries in Coventry's history was made. Archaeologists unearthed 17 Iron Age roundhouses, part of a larger settlement dating to betweem 100 BC and AD 100. As certain soil levels had already been removed finds were limited and included pieces of pottery and an Iron Age lamp. It has been suggested that the area may have been settled from the Neolithic period and is a reminder of our area's lost prehistory, more of which still awaits discovery.

Further Reading
Canley Woodlands, Parks & Leisure Dept, Coventry Leisure Services leaflet.
Mary Dormer Harris, *Some Manors, Churches and Villages of Warwickshire*, 1937.
Sir William Dugdale, *Warwickshire*, 1817.
Newspapers and scrapbooks, Local Studies.

Chapelfields

Fragments of Roman pottery were found in Chapelfields in Broomfield Road in 1896. What the Romans were doing in the area we do not know, but finds from these times are not uncommon around the city.

Chapelfields itself takes its name from 'the chapel in the fields', a reference to the leper's chapel and hospital that stood around the junction of Hearsall Lane and the Allesley Old Road. The origins of the hospital go back to the 12th century when Hugh de Kevilok, Earl of Chester and lord of Coventry, promised to join a crusade to the Holy Land. Finding himself unable to keep the promise he sent a friend, William de Auney, in his stead.

De Auney served his master with valour and honour, but before returning home contracted leprosy, one of the most feared diseases of the mediaeval world. When he returned he could not attend his lord for fear of infecting him, causing the great lord some distress. To do right by de Auney Earl Kevilok built him a house far enough from Coventry to allay people's fear of infection, but near enough for him to be at hand. Here in the mediaeval wasteland William de Auney was cared for until he took his last breath.

At around the time of de Auney's death Earl Kevilok extended the property, turning it into a hospital and adding a chapel dedicated to St Leonard. His charter stated it would be 'for the maintenance of such lepers as should happen to be in Coventry.' The hospital and chapel were attended by a priest and a special fraternity of brothers and sisters, who cared for the inmates both medically and by the power of prayer.

By 1280 the chapel of St Leonard and its hospital had ceased to be used for lepers and it became a royal free chapel dedicated to St Mary Magdalene. The chapel and hospital were then acquired by Coventry Priory and in the reign of Edward IV came into the hands of the King, who passed them onto the Cannons of Studley, on condition that they prayed for the monarch and his family.

After Henry VIII's Dissolution most of the buildings were demolished and the chapel turned into a barn for a local farm. Over the years it gradually fell into ruins. Over time much of the stonework was taken from the site but in 1847 when the land was being cleared carved stones and statues could still be seen half-buried and scattered around the site. Workmen unearthed many pieces of carving and numerous skeletons. The statues were taken by Alderman Phillips, a collector of antiquities who placed them in his garden in Little Park Street.

A writer in 1942 says of Chapelfields in the old days:

> *Passing under the railway viaduct we come to 'Chapel' Fields. Fifty or sixty years ago (1890s) this was invariably called, 'The Land'. … Just inside Hearsall Lane where Broomfield Place is now, was a pad, the 'Black Pad,'* [means the black pathway] *a narrow path which led into the Butts, very close to where the*

Shops on the Allesley Old Road in 1935.

Technical College now stands ... The houses on the left-hand side of Hearsall Lane were not built then; it was all open ground up to Hearsall Common, except for a farm on that side.

The first real building on the land around the Chapelfields area, then part of Spon End, was Chapelfields House and nursery garden at the beginning of the 19th century. The site was called Weare's Nursery and lay on Thomas White charity land. Thomas Weare, a nurseryman and seedsman, had a shop in Broadgate and it is because of him that the Nursery Tavern got its name. In 1845 an Act of Parliament empowered the trustees of the charity to 'lay out roads and sell plots by public auction for development.' Those who sought to move to The Land were mainly the watchmakers who had spread from the city into crowded Spon End and the Butts.

In 1846 Craven Street, Duke Street, Lord Street and Mount Street were laid out on the fields and lots began to be sold: Chapelfields was born. By June the following year 16 houses had been erected in Duke and Craven Street and by 1851 70 houses were built and under occupation and soon there was a thriving community of watchmakers, journeymen and masters set within this new village in the fields. Plots were still being sold in 1880 since Joseph Evans, a watch gilder, sold William Hulm, a watchmaker, two roped plots in Lord Street, numbered 29 and 30 in May of that year for £250. Two houses and gardens, numbers 30 and 31, were also included in the price, both of which included outbuildings built by watchmaker Thomas Hill who had died five years earlier. Thankfully a large number of these watchmaker's houses survive, along with the pubs (seven in four streets) that quenched the watchmakers' thirst.

Oxford Terrace was built on the site of the leper's hospital facing the Allesley Old Road. It consisted of two master's houses, which still stand. The first master's house and factory belonged to Philip Cohen, whose workers produced complete 'superior quality' watches until 1901. Many watchmen only produced parts — cases, dials, and so on — which were passed on by child runners to other artisans, who would eventually produce the complete watch, often with a works imported from Prescot. In 1901 William Neal took over the premises and produced gold watchcases until 1931. The frontages of these buildings are well-built houses hiding the factories behind and few who passed

Two of the many watchmakers' houses in Chapelfields.

down the Allesley Old Road and were not locals would know that this was an industrial settlement.

In the early 20th century it was still possible to stand at Chapelfields and look north across open countryside down to Radford village on the Radford Road. The land was mainly farmland, much of it in the Chapelfields district being farmed by the Green family. Many still remember farmer Green taking his cattle through the local streets.

Albert Peck recalls that in 1941 Prince of Wales Road ended at No.165. Beyond this the land still belonged to the Thomas White's charity estate and was farmed by farmer Green. In around 1952 the land was purchased by T.P. Smith Ltd and laid out for building. Albert moved into his house, which had been the site of a searchlight battery in 1955.

During the war the area between Prince of Wales Road and Lake View Road consisted mainly of allotments. Much wartime rubble from the city centre was dumped there. Later, after the allotments were given up, the land was levelled, seeded and made into parkland. A lake was planned but never happened and Lake View Road must now be the only road in the country to bear such a name and have no actual lake view.

Further Reading
J. Foulds, J. Beever and P. Robinson, *Memories of Chapelfields and Hearsall*, Vols 1 & 2.
The Coventry Watchmaker's Heritage Trail, Coventry Watch Museum Project, 2001.
Newspaper cuttings, Local Studies.

CHEYLESMORE

The earliest known spelling is 'Chilsmore', from 1249. The following year the modern spelling Cheylesmore first appears. It is thought to have derived from the early English '*cielde*' meaning well or spring, and '*mor*' meaning moor. Some believe the spring in question was the Baron's Well, which stood in Cheylesmore Park. This ancient well has no known history but interestingly the water from it flowed through the mouth of an ancient weatherworn stone face. This is highly suggestive of a Roman or Celtic pagan well. The moorland beyond the well was said to be very wet up to the time of Henry VIII, containing, 'Mottes and waters on every side.'

The manor of Cheylesmore originated with Leofric and Godiva, before passing into the hands of the earls of Chester, the last of whom, Ranulf Blundeville, died in 1232. The estate passed to the Earl of Arundel through his marriage to Ranulf's sister Mabel. It is said that in around 1237 he built Cheylesmore Manor House with a moat and park to replace the redundant Coventry Castle. The manor then passed to the 5th earl, who died in 1243, then to Lord Roger de Montalt and his wife Cicely.

In 1249 Roger and Cicely agreed to rent Cheylesmore, with the southern portion of Coventry known as the Manor of Cheylesmore, to Coventry Priory for £107 a year, plus 10 marks to the nuns of Polesworth. This did not include the manor house and park.

In 1327 the land and house were still in the hands of the Montalts and Robert and Emma Montalt agreed that if Robert died without an heir the manor would revert to Queen Isabella. This happened in 1330 and later the estate passed to her grandson, Edward of Woodstock, the Black Prince, who stayed at the manor house on his way back to London after his grandmother's death. Indeed, although we have no historic documents to prove it, it is said Edward often hunted deer in Cheylesmore Park and that in 1362 he had the park enclosed with palings.

After Edward's death the park passed to his son, Richard II (reigned 1377–99), who had the city wall diverted to encompass the building. Cheylesmore Park at the time was said to be around 436 acres in extent, consisting of pasture, woodland and moor, inhabited by deer and other game. The park's keeper was one Thomas de Quinton, who took or gave his name to Quinton Pool, near which he probably lived. It was up to Thomas to make sure the royal deer had enough grazing, by managing the land. It is also claimed that Quinton Pool may have taken its name from the mediaeval jousting game

Quinton Pool as it appeared in 1946, reflecting the spires of St Michael and Holy Trinity. (CCL)

A 19th century etching showing Coventry as seen from a now enclosed Cheylesmore Park.

'quintain,' which may have taken place nearby. Water quintain might even have been played in the pool itself.

Many years later Edward VI granted the manor and park to John Dudley, Earl of Warwick, who as Duke of Northumberland leased the manor to the Corporation on the condition that 80 cows and 20 geldings belonging to the poor were pastured there. In the 17th century the manor reverted to Charles I and in 1660 the mayor and aldermen turned over the manor and park to the newly installed Charles II. He, remembering the city's snub to his father during the Civil War, granted the lease to Sir Thomas Townsend. Townsend lived at the manor house until 1685 when it was made into tenements. The Corporation obtained the lease in 1727, with freemen having pasture rights. In 1787 when the lease ended it was acquired from the Prince of Wales by Lord Beauchamp. The following April he directed that the double row of trees in the park, a favourite place for promenading, be cut down. In 1788 the park and manor house were the property of William Preest, and during his tenancy in 1795 a survey was made that measured the park at 465 acres, one rod and two perches. Preest had turned the area nearest the city wall into allotments and further south he enclosed parts of the park into fields. The rest was used for the inhabitants of Coventry to graze cattle. The royal connection ended in 1819 when the Prince of Wales sold the estate to the Marquis of Hertford and in 1871 it came to H.W. Eaton, Lord Cheylesmore. Thereafter the land was gradually sold and built upon during the 20th century, beginning with the area nearest the city centre.

The actual manor house was excavated a few years ago and found to be a long building with a sandstone base. The sandstone would have reached first window level, above which the structure would have been timbered. The gateway to the large square courtyard still stands and is now the Coventry Registry Office. The main building was still standing in 1659 and was referred to as the 'mansion house called Cheylesmore Mannor House, with the barns, stables, outhouses, orchards, gardens.' Part of this manor house appears to have stood until the 20th century, because a large building attached to the gateway, which had been converted into flats, had 'magnificent roof timbers' brought to light by bomb damage. The building was demolished in 1955.

There was a watermill in the park called Cheylesmore Mill, which was described in 1659 as an overshoot fulling mill at Quinton with a dwelling house in the occupation of Henry Gamm. Quinton Pool itself was the mill-pool. Quinton also became a significant place in 1625–6, for the City annals record that plague came to the city. Many inhabitants fled and occupied buildings erected on the Greyfriars Orchard and near Quinton Pool in the park.

William Odell wrote in the 19th century of his memories of Cheylesmore in the late 18th century:

A great deal of Cheylesmore Royal Park was enclosed just before my memory begins; still I remember a great deal of it being open. It was much used by people in Little Park Street and Dead Lane. My father remembered the park being all open, and down to Whitley and Quinton — a wild place, abounding with gorse. Previously to the 5th November in his day lads used to fetch in any quantities they pleased; neither did they stop here, for they used with impunity to cut off arms and branches of trees.

What is now called the 'Mount Tree' standing in the Park, but near to Whitley Common, was the last tree of a double row commencing at Little Park Street.

The avenue of trees planted by the mayor in 1625 from the Park Hollows where the martyrs were burned was chopped down in the early 19th century and the Mount Tree, said to have been planted to commemorate Charles I attacking the city, was felled by a storm. According to the city annals the mount, which stood adjacent to the tree, was raised in 1627 and trees planted on it. The mount was later said to have been where Charles I set up his tent during the siege of Coventry in 1642. Interestingly on the edge of the Park, on a junction between the London Road, the Whitley Causeway (now London Road) and an unnamed track, stood the Old Windmill Hill, a huge raised hill, which stood near the present lodge in London Road Cemetery. The mound can be seen on Samuel Bradford's map of 1748 and shows the hill standing alone on what must have been fairly flat ground. This is curious, because although there was once a windmill on the mound, why would anyone go to the trouble of raising such a massive mound for a windmill?

William Odell continued his reminiscences:

There was two Parks, 'Great' and 'Little,' but no division of them [In 1659 the Great Park was 480 acres and Little Park 25 acres] that I remember. It used to be a favourite walk of the citizens, and bowling and other games were enjoyed there. The local Militia and Volunteers, in my youth, went in for daily exercise and training.

Near Quarryfield Road and Puma Road stood the winning post of Coventry Races, said to have first been run in the Park in 1755, although the winning post can be seen on Bradford's map of 1748–9. The first major race recorded as taking place in the Great Park on 12 August 1755, when the first race for £50 was won by a grey called Maggot. The following year Lord Byron's grey hunter, Lightening,

The gateway house to Cheylesmore Manor, photographed in 1892, dates to the 14th century and was restored in the 1960s, becoming the oldest registry office in the country. The building behind, later converted into flats, contained parts of the original manor house and a splendid mediaeval roof. It was demolished in the 1950s.

The Martyrs Memorial by Mile Lane, Cheylesmore. The memorial, dedicated in 1910, was moved a short distance to its present site during the building of the ring road. Some 200 yards from its present position the Coventry martyrs were burned for their beliefs in the Park Hollows.

came third in a race. The races ended in the Park in 1783 when a rider lost control of his horse, which jumped a stile at Little Park Gate and killed a seven-year-old girl.

The development of Cheylesmore really began with the building of industrial premises, housing and Mile Lane School around the Parkside area. Notable firms were sited here such as Armstrong Siddeley Motors, which produced cars, gears and aero and tank engines from 1901, and Maudslay and Swift, which moved in in 1906. Beeston also produced a tri-car at the Mile Lane/Quinton Road factory (later home to Swift) in 1896, which was Britain's only entry in that year's Emancipation Run. The firm started to produce true four-wheeled motor cars in 1898. The land continued to be

Cheylesmore's main shopping centre, Quinton Parade, in around 1950. (CCL)

developed towards Quinton from the late 1920s onwards and the Quinton area belongs mainly to the post-war period, leaving a much smaller Quinton Pool on open ground the only reminder of the great royal hunting park of Cheylesmore.

Before leaving the district there are two stories connected to Quinton Pool. The first, taken from a rhyme, tells that the pool was home to a great dragon in ancient times. It would walk to Cheylesmore Gate where it was placated by being fed damsels. Coventry's St George was called in to put an end to the great beast.

Another story from the early 19th century was recalled in the 1930s for a Coventry newspaper by a 93-year-old lady. She recalled a story her grandmother used to tell her when she was a small child:

My grandmother lived in a cottage near to the pool, with her mother; a lady of nearly eighty years. There were many rats around the old cottage, and one of them used to come inside. He became friendly and very, very tame. The old lady called him Canopus. He used to sit in front of the old lady's feet and watch her knitting, and in fact watched her every movement, but never attempted to approach nearer than a respectful distance. He used to look up at her and she used to say she could tell exactly what Canopus was thinking, and a very deep friendship existed between them.

Later the old lady became ill and had to keep to her room upstairs. Canopus would quietly climb the stairs, scramble on to a stool beside the bed and watch the old lady, who felt comforted by his presence there. Eventually the old lady died but Canopus continued to come into the cottage looking for her, no one could see him but heard his footsteps. The old cottage was repaired and despite the workman swearing no rat could get into the building Canopus' footsteps could be heard every night as he searched the cottage for his old friend.

Further Reading
Frederick Bliss Burbidge, *Old Coventry and Lady Godiva*.
Museum of British Road Transport, *Coventry Car Factories: A Centenary Guide*.
Newspapers and cuttings, Local Studies.

COUNDON

Place-name experts cannot make up their minds about the origin of the name Coundon. It has been said that the earliest spelling was 'Cunedawrwlym', which is said to be from the Anglo-Saxon, meaning 'a boiling up of waters, a spring or head of a river.' This does make some sense, for within the parish is Coundon Spring, which in the 19th century was recorded as pumping out up to 100,000 gallons of water a day. This water fed the Washbrook, which crosses Northbrook Road just below the original village centre. There is a suggestion that the name has a Celtic origin, since the word 'cune' means a hound in that language. Duignan, a place-name expert, thought the name came from the Gaulish language and meant a confluence of streams. Other sources suggest it means 'the settlement on the hill', part of the word meaning hill escarpment, and the original village does lie on top of rising ground. Another suggested origin of the name, that it means 'the settlement by the Cune' makes little sense. The River Cune, now the Sherbourne, passes well below the old settlement site.

The lower section of Coundon, previously the site of Alvis Motors and now the Alvis Retail Park, was the scene of some interest in 1926 when a hippopotamus skull was unearthed. The 80,000-year-old skull was in good condition and still had its lower jaw, suggesting that the animal had died there and not been swept there by glacial movement. It was found 15ft down in interglacial gravel and was saved from destruction by two men, one of whom was the archaeologist J.H. Edwards, who donated it to a museum. The animal's skeleton apparently also survived and was reburied.

The suggestion that the name Coundon denotes a Celtic settlement is backed by a find in Coundon Green in the 1990s of a piece of a Celtic horse bridle bit dating from the late 1st century

A pristine housing estate photographed in Coundon in the 1920s. (CCL)

BC to the early 1st century AD, showing the passage of a Celtic chariot through the area. The same area also yielded a silver serrated denarius struck in 80 BC, long before the Roman invasion. A sestertius of Antoninus Pius dating to the mid-2nd century was found in Sherbourne Crescent, and a bronze coin of Constantine I has also been found in Coundon.

A John Gulson drawing of old pollarded oaks in Coundon in 1849. (CCL)

The oldest standing structure in the district is St Catherine's Well in Beaumont Crescent (off the Holyhead Road). Here in the curve of a suburban 1930s street stands a raised chapel-like structure covering a well, which once stood on a grassy knoll in open fields. Dating back to the early 1400s, the origins of St Catherine's Well are lost in the mists of time, but stories connected to it suggest pagan origins. One story relates that there is a secret passage or cavern under the well, which may come from the ancient folk belief that wells and water were entrances to the other worlds.

Ancient wells and springs were sacred in the pre-Christian period and were usually attended by a keeper who lived in a cell next to the well. Interestingly, when the site was revamped in the early 1930s the remains of a small building were unearthed, although this could also have been a shrine.

Sometime in the early 1400s St Catherine's Well was probably re-dug, converted into a conduit and crowned with its chapel-like structure and given its dedication to a Christian saint. This appears to have been done by the Priory of St Mary in Coventry, as in the Pittancer's Rental of the priory of 1410–11, a small heath is mentioned 'in which the conduit of the aforesaid Prior and Convent now lies.' The fact that the church owned both this and other conduits around the city does not mean that they supplied the priory with water, as there were many springs above and below the priory site. One found in the 1930s pumped water from the sandstone rock into hollow oak logs, which acted as pipes. St Catherine's Well appears to have fed only Spon End, and possibly part of Spon Street, and continued to supply 100,000 gallons a day until it ran dry in 1847.

Coundon was granted by Earl Leofric to the monks of St Mary's, Coventry, in 1042. One of the few Coventry villages mentioned in the Domesday Survey, it is referred to as 'Condelme' and two holdings are

A John Gulson drawing from 1849 of a Coundon lane. (CCL)

noted, one held by Roger, who was a tenant of William Fitzcorbucion. He had one plough of arable land, worked by two people, and woodland measuring nearly three quarters of a mile. The rest belonged to the prior of Coventry and consisted of two ploughs and a considerable amount of woodland. Eleven people worked the prior's holding, including one slave.

The Golden Nugget in Coundon is said to have been started with the proceeds from a golden nugget from the Californian goldfields in the 19th century. The pub was a popular stopping point for drovers on their way to Coventry.

Dugdale records that in the time of Henry III (1216–1272) the monks of Coventry held court leet in the village and had a gallows and assize of bread and beer. The gallows site may have been in Scots Lane, which was once known as Hangman's Lane, although a 1675 boundary list states that the site of Coundon Gallows was on the corner of Keresley Heath. Coundon must have once had a chapel, although the 12th-century charter of Ranulf Gernon, Earl of Chester, does not mention it, and no other historical documents record it. However, pieces of stonework in the grounds of Coundon Court School are definitely remains of an ancient ecclesiastical building of the 14th century, and local tradition claims that there was once a monastic building on the site.

The Bennett family of Allesley were the main tenants throughout the mediaeval period. Their name is preserved in Bennetts Road in Keresley, as the family also held land in the north of Keresley. During the reign of Henry III (1207–72), John Bennett was the tenant on land held by Henry de Hastings, who was the heir to the Corbucion estate. In 1410 the bounds were defined as Old and New Coundon, with Coundon Green in the prior's holding and a boundary hedge called Bennetts Hedge diving it from the de Hasting estate heading towards Allesley.

After the Dissolution in 1542 the prior's holding, which was worked from his farm, Moat House Farm (near the junction of Brownshill Green and Norman Place roads), passed to Richard Andrews and Leonard Chamberlain. This land was later part of the Thomas White charity estate and other charity estates. In 1529 the farm was mentioned in an 80-year lease for a yearly rent of £17 13s 4d for the 'Mothouse' with an orchard, garden, croft, field and diverse other pieces of land and tithes of wool and lamb. Thomas Camswell, prior of Coventry, gave the lease over to Michael Bolde. In 1604, Dr Wilkes, the King's Chaplain, held the farm, followed by the Clarke family in the latter part of the century. The farm survived into the 20th century as Manor House Farm. In 1927 the farmland began to be built on and in 1931 Manor House Farm was demolished.

Land was leased here by the Bohuns from 1574. Ralph Bohun, on his death in 1632, is said to have had a large house and other property in Coundon. In the 18th century the family were still acquiring land here and in 1730 it passed through marriage to Gilbert Clerk.

Mediaeval names survive in the area, such as the Holifast Waste, remembered in Hollyfast Lane; Brownshill Green Road was in existence before 1411 and was known as the Maxstoke Way. In 1410 there were 18 tenants on the estate, a fraction of the number a few years earlier, probably due to plague. The ancient centre of the village never grew and a scattering of houses formed the district in 1730 when there were only 15 houses in Coundon.

In 1850 the directory records 220 inhabitants in the scattered area of Coundon. Stephen Barnwell, a ribbon manufacturer, is noted as residing at the Villa, and at Coundon Green lived Stephen Knapp, a printer. The Revd James Henry Mapleton lived at the vicarage opposite Keresley Grange. Mr and Mrs Elizabeth King lived at Coundon House and David Waters, a spirit merchant of Waters of Coventry, occupied a house called Oakhurst. Those who farmed the largely rural area were George Hands, William Lee of Lower Coundon Farm, John Sammons of Coundon Cottages, Arthur Startin and James Sibley Whittem, who also owned the Moat House in Wyken.

The directory of 1874 reports that the population had fallen to 201 and Coundon House was occupied by Major Richard Caldicott. John Cash of the noted Cash's weaving family now resided at the vicarage (they later moved to the Moat House, Keresley), while John Rotherham, a watch manufacturer, lived at Cedar Cottage, which now stands next to Coundon Court. Many of the area's inhabitants lived in Coundon but worked in Coventry, like Thomas Jenkins, a druggist at Coventry, and William Ratcliffe, a brewer at Coventry, who resided at the Cottage. The only retailers and workers in the area apart from farmers were Thomas Green who ran the beer house, possibly what became the Nugget in Coundon Green, purchased so the story goes with gold from the Australian goldfields, John Sanders, a tailor, and Joseph Sparrow, the blacksmith and agricultural implement maker. The railway, in the lower part of the parish on Coundon Road, was manned by James Robertson, stationmaster.

St Catherine's Well, bearing its early 15th-century chapel-like top, photographed in the Conduit Meadow in around 1900.

Coundon became a centre for Coventry's well-to-do business families in the 19th and early 20th century. David Shakespeare Waters, who set up Waters of Coventry, Wine & Spirit Merchants, traded in Coventry and the

Coundon Court, now Coundon Court School, was built by Coventry industrialist and mayor George Singer.

High Street for nearly 200 years. He probably bought the large Georgian house called Oakhurst in Coundon to retire there. However, his son David took up residence there in 1844 after his marriage. When his father died in 1849 (the family grave can still be seen at Keresley Church), he moved back to the family and business premises in High Street, Coventry.

Richard Caldicott was a member of the well-known silk manufacturing family. He moved into Coundon House (Southbank Road), which then stood in open countryside, and carried on with the family business, as a silk merchant. He lived a varied lifestyle and travelled the world. Having no children he left the house to his nephew. After his death the estate was purchased by the late Mr William Coker Iliffe (elder brother of Lord Iliffe), who later sold parts of it for housing development.

During the latter part of the 20th century Coundon House, which is thought to date from the 17th century, stood semi-derelict and vandalised. It was recently restored and turned into exclusive apartments. Other large residences are Coundon Court, built on Coundon Farm land by cycle manufacturer George Singer in 1891. The following year he was made mayor of Coventry. Singer died suddenly in 1909 and his widow Eliza had the house auctioned in 1912. It became the home of Captain Charles Miller, then passed to the Finns, who sold the house to Coventry Corporation in 1953 for £15,000. The house was converted into a girl's school and opened with 120 girls in 1954. It became a mixed school in the early 1970s and is now one of the city's best comprehensive schools.

Coundon Hall appears to date from around 1800. The owner of the hall until October 1821 was John Hopkin. He died without an heir and the hall and its surrounds were sold by auction. In the

20th century the owners were the Turrall family. Mr Turrall's hobby was cattle and he kept Herefords and white longhorns that would wander around what is now Coundon Hall Park.

A well-known place of mass entertainment in Coundon is the Coundon Road Ground, home of rugby union. The first match was held on the ground on 12 March 1921 and was started by the mayor, Councillor Grant, who put boot to leather. The match did not go in Coventry's favour and the United Services side from Portsmouth won 13–3. The day's take was £242, over half what had been paid for the site. The biggest crowd was said to be 18,000 at an England and Wales schools international. In 1945 Cardiff ended Coventry's 63 match unbeaten record in front of a crowd of 15,000. Since opening more than 100 first-class clubs have played at the ground and they continue to do so in 2003.

On the Holyhead Road by the railway bridge stood the first Coundon factory, set up by T.G. John and called the Alvis. Here castings and small engines were made and the first car, a 10.7hp Alvis, emerged in 1920. In 1935 the company built another large factory on the other side of the bridge (the present Alvis Retail Park) and continued producing cars such as the Crested Eagle. Before and during the war armoured vehicles and aero engines were made, and the firm continued to produce them in peace time. The last car, a 3-litre Mark IV in the TF 21 series, left the production line on 20 August 1967. The factory was demolished in 1990.

In the late 18th century a hamlet developed in Coundon and Allesley at Brownshill Green, below the smithy, which stood in Wall Hill Road (just down from Coundon Wedge Road). In *Just Amongst Ourselves* Mrs Wharton recalls:

> *We seemed to have more snow and frost years ago than we do now. There was no road gritting in those days so people, who like my father depended on a horse and cart for business, had to make an early visit to the blacksmith, Mr Sparrow, at Brownshill Green. This was to have the horses' shoes roughened, which meant having extra nails in the shoes to grip the road.*

Coventry Station on Coundon Road in around 1905. Although the station is no longer used this view remains unchanged. (CCL)

The Tithe Map of 1844 shows Brownshill Green, Coundon, as being a small scattering of buildings around a large open expanse of grass with the lower part of the present Wall Hill Road and Hawkes Mill Lane being simply dirt tracks through the open green. In 1850 the small hamlet of Brownshill Green was farmed by Henry Taylor, Richard Terry, William Barr, who was a wheelwright but also a farmer,

57

and Robert Warden, who kept cows. John Smith was the blacksmith and William Beacham kept a shop, while Thomas Beacham kept the beer house.

In 1874 a village shop was in the hands of William Barr, who was previously described as a wheelwright and farmer. William Beacham, who held the shop previously, was now a carter. A second shop was held by Henry Sheasby, while Joseph Sparrow worked the smithy. William Barr died on 7 November 1878 leaving

Brownshill Green as it appeared in 2003. The road in the centre originally ran through an open green with ridge and furrow fields surrounding it, some of which can still be seen. The house on the left is early to mid-19th century and beyond stands the garage, for many years the site of the village smithy.

his wife Mary Ann; he was described in his will as a wheelwright. William left his wife the Rose public house in Brownshill Green, Allesley, which he had recently purchased from Stephen Saidler. He left his stepdaughter Sarah Jane Minstrell other properties in Brownshill Green. His own house passed to his stepson Thomas. In the will, dated 1872, William Barr signed with a cross because he was illiterate.

The only remaining inn in Brownshill Green is the White Lion, which was originally a Victorian cottage called the Laurels, home to the Skermer family. Herbert Skermer and his wife originally ran an off-licence from the back of the house and later obtained a full licence and converted the cottage into a pub.

One of the most notorious events to happen in Brownshill Green occurred on 6 January 1817, when someone entered the dwelling of George Rogers of Brownshill Green, Allesley and 'inhumanely murdered the said George Rogers by cutting his Throat and fracturing his Skull.' The murderer ransacked the house and took silver teaspoons, two gold wedding rings, an ivory box marked 'GR', a shirt and breeches, probably because of the blood on his clothes, and a joint of bacon. A reward offering £50 was placed in the *Coventry Standard* by William Garlick, the constable of Allesley, and it was not long before the murderer, a man called Charles Sanders, was taken. He was hanged in April outside Warwick Gaol.

Further Reading
Keresley Women's Institute, *Just Amongst Ourselves*.
John Ashby, *The History of Long Lane*, 1994. Paper in Local Studies.
Victoria County History, Vol. 8.
Nat Alcock & Robert Caldicott, *Waters of Coventry*, 2002.
Various newspapers, Local Studies.

EARLSDON

The earliest known spelling is from a Letters Patent of Edward, the Black Prince, dated 1364, which refers to the area as the 'Aylesdene' and the 'field of Aylesdene'. 'Ayles' is from the Anglo-Saxon personal name Aegal, and 'dene' means valley, so the name would mean Aegal's valley. The district was farmland throughout much of its history, and in the 1830s John Moore, a Coventry farmer

Earlsdon Street photographed in around 1910 showing 'Ma Cooper's' on the left. (CCL)

and butcher, built a new farmhouse off what became Moor Street on an area called the Six Fields. The 31-acre estate was sold in 1852 to the Coventry Freehold Land Society. It lay between Elsdon Lane (Earlsdon Avenue) and Whor Lane (Beechwood Avenue) and the society laid it out as eight streets with plots for self-building. This was the beginning of Elsdon or Earlsdon village.

The streets marked out were Moor Street, Earlsdon Street, Earlsdon Terrace, Providence Street, Cromwell Street, Clarendon Street, Arden Street and Warwick Street. Water and drainage were laid on and in 1852 John Flinn, a watch manufacturer from Prescot, built the first house, Earlsdon House, which still stands in Warwick Street. Attached to the back of the substantial double-fronted villa was a workshop where 14 men and five boys were employed in watchmaking. Flinn moved back to

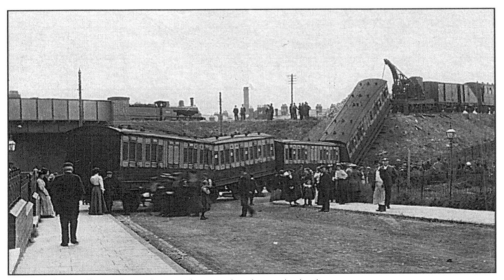

A train derailment in Albany Road on 2 July 1904. The crane on the track was used to drag the carriages back up onto the rails. (CCL)

Coventry in 1868 and sold the house and factory to Joseph White, considered by many to be Earlsdon's most outstanding watchmaker. Flinn had a row of 13 cottages, called Flinn's Cottages, built in Arden Street for his workers.

A mid-19th century engraving looking from the railway cutting in Earlsdon Lane (now Earlsdon Avenue) towards Coventry. (CCL.)

Growth continued at a slow pace and by 1854 only 10 houses had been built. This rose to 107 by 1861. The watch trade employed 146 men, but by 1894 there were still only 187 families in the village. The take up rate was slow because the area was thought to be a watchmaker's suburb, and watchmakers were artisans who were said to consider themselves above the likes of weavers, some of whom initially took up residence in Cromwell Street. The area had also gained a reputation for undesirables and lay along an open sewer, which ran alongside the 'jetty' and drained into the Sherbourne. This open ditch was particularly smelly in summer and in winter often overflowed.

Real development did not start until the opening of the Albany Road by the Duchess of Albany in December 1898. Thereafter buildings spread towards the Kenilworth Road and Canley. By the latter years of the 19th century larger villas were being built for the more affluent Victorian middle

The Earlsdon Drug Stores in 1908. They were run by Arthur Hoyle at No.2, Earlsdon Street.

classes, in contrast to the smaller terraced houses built for the working classes in the north of the parish. The village was swallowed by the city and filled with people of all trades. From the watchmaking days comes the expression Coventrians used against Earlsdonites, that they were all 'brown boots and no breakfast,' meaning they were snobby, as they always had a pair of brown boots to wear on a Sunday (black for working) despite the fact that some had to go without breakfasts to afford them.

Earlsdon's pubs were and still are popular places, the most famous being the City Arms, affectionately remembered as, 'Ma Cooper's' after Mary Jane Cooper, who took over the running of the pub in 1896 until her death in 1921. The original Victorian pub was demolished in 1930, rebuilt in a mock-Tudor style, and remains a popular venue. The Earlsdon Cottage Inn's first landlord was Joseph Aston Atkins, a watch motioner by trade who decided shortly before the 1871 census to turn his house, which he built in 1855, into a pub. Earlsdon's third pub is the Royal Oak, in Earlsdon Street, which was opened by John Sabin in 1859. These three pubs are known throughout Coventry, being particularly popular with serious ale drinkers and students.

One of Coventry's most famous sons was born in Earlsdon. Frank Whittle was born at 72, Newcombe Road, in 1907, and he attended the local school, where he earned the nickname 'Mr Brains'. As a young boy he saw his first aeroplane while crossing Hearsall Common. The plane was so low it blew his cap from his head into a nearby gorse bush. This sparked an interest in aircraft and as a young man he entered the RAF as a flying cadet at Cranfield, where he got a reputation for being a 'crazy flyer,' because he loved to perform dangerous stunts. In 1929 while back in Coventry, living in Regent Street near the city centre, Frank first conceived the idea of using a gas turbine to build a jet engine and in 1937 he tested his first experimental jet engine at Rugby. On 15 May 1941 the first test flight of a Gloster E28 powered by two Whittle jet engines took place and within a short time speeds of up to 370mph were reached. Three years later news of Britain's jet fighter was announced to the world. Frank Whittle, the son of an Earlsdon factory foreman, became Sir Frank in 1948 and thereafter was known as the 'Father of the Jet Engine', the man who shrank the world.

Much of Hearsall Common lies within Earlsdon, apart from an area around Guphill Ford, which used to lie in the manor of Stoneleigh. Hearsall is first mentioned in 1232 as 'Hetheshal', which is believed to be derived from the Old English, '*haedes heale*' meaning the corner of the heath. In the 14th century Hearsall lay between Whoberley Fields and Whorwell or Horwell, which Dugdale suggests was a depopulated village. Parish records up to the 18th century often refer to 'Hearsall alias Whorwell', suggesting that if there was a lost settlement it would have been at Hearsall, along Whor Lane (Beechwood Avenue) and near the Whor Brook.

In the early 18th century a windmill stood on the common, where there were grazing rights for city freemen. At the Broad Lane end the track across the common was gated to stop the freemen's cattle from wandering beyond the common. The freemen's rights to the common were reduced in 1860 and further reduced in 1875 by the council, which paid the freemen a yearly sum in compensation. In 1927 the council finally stopped grazing rights on Hearsall Common.

The common was a place of entertainment and in 1581 it was recorded that there was a wrestling place there. In the 18th and 19th century it was a regular venue for prize fighting. Not all of the common could be grazed for much consisted of trees, bushes and gorse. Joseph Gutteridge wrote of his memories of Hearsall early in the 19th century:

Looking across the edge of Hearsall Common and Hearsall Lane to Queensland Avenue in the early 1930s.

My father would take me into the country to visit his brother, a schoolmaster at Berkswell. We had to cross Hearsall Common. It was at that time but ill-fitted for its purpose as grazing land for the freeman's cattle. Except for the highway that passed over it, and a few patches of grass, it was a mass of gorse and fern. To me it was a very paradise with its gorse bushes redundant with vivid yellow blossom, and the tall and strong-ribbed fronds of the brake fern ... Here and there were patches of broom, which furnished masses of golden flowers, and the intervals between the bushes were carpeted with ling, purple with blossom. Upon the waste pieces delicate harebell ... blossomed plentifully ...

The common was alive with wildlife including the sand and green lizard. The common was also popular with the local watchmakers, who would often cross it on a Sunday morning on their walks to Berkswell to sup ale at the Bear.

Those who traversed the common sometimes did so at their own risk, as the *Coventry Mercury* of 30 September 1768 recorded:

William Nailer was placed in Coventry Gaol as a result of his assaulting and attempting to rob, Joseph Clifton on the night of September 29th, upon Hearsall Common. Nailer was sentenced to death at Coventry Assizes, August 6th 1768 for robbing Richard Phillips in the Six Close, near Coventry of 4/8d during July.

In 1833 we are informed that at the bottom of the common stood the Hawthorn Tree public house, which stood just below the beech wood from which the present Beechwood Avenue takes its name. Here in October women gathering wood discovered the grisly remains of a suicide who had put his hat on his

A tram passing under the bridge in Albany Road, Earlsdon, in the early 1930s.

Looking down Earlsdon Street in around 1932.

stick and literally decapitated himself with a razor. The body had been there for some time, and 'the head was a short distance from the body and the flesh completely eaten from every part of it by vermin.' The inquest held at the Hawthorn concluded that he had killed himself while insane.

From 1895 part of the common was used as a golf course until it moved to Beechwood Avenue in 1907 and in the 1950s the great fair was accommodated by levelling the western end of the common. A large area which had been levelled in 1860 by unemployed weavers was made into sports pitches, leaving the original common mostly untouched across the road.

Another open area of recreation within the parish was Spencer Park. Originally the park was to be on Stivichall Common but difficulties were had obtaining the land and the project was abandoned. David Spencer, a draper from Greyfriars Green, had originally offered the council 4,000 guineas to fund the park, and one day when he was walking with the mayor and town clerk they noticed a large meadow, on part of which the new Henry VIII School was to be built, and decided this would be the ideal place. The 'Gymnasium' was opened in 1894, consisting of swings, a roundabout, a seesaw and a slide, and in 1915 a bowling green and tennis courts were opened. The park was always a popular place, not only for recreation but also for gatherings and parades.

The east of the district was originally called Asthill, meaning the ash hill, and is commemorated by Asthill Grove and Asthill Road. Dugdale said that Asthill was totally depopulated and in his time was only remembered by a thicket of trees called Asthill Grove.

Further Reading
Mary Montes, *Earlsdon Heritage Trail*, 2000.
Mary Montes, *Earlsdon Take Two*, 1986.
Mary Montes, *Brown Boots in Earlsdon*, 1989.
Memories of Chapelfields and Hearsall, Vols I and 2.

EXHALL

Exhall is technically within the bounds of Bedworth, but as it is attached to modern Coventry and is mentioned in the early charters of Coventry it appears here. The name is traditionally from the Saxon, meaning 'Aecca's hall,' the hall of Ecca, although more recently it has been identified as deriving from 'Ecceles Healh', meaning the 'church nook', or 'Eccel's nook'. Nothing is recorded in the Domesday Book regarding Exhall, and it may have been part of the Foleshill and Ansty districts at that time. The first mention of the village is in a charter granted in the 12th century by Ranulf Gernon, Earl of Chester, giving the monks of Coventry certain grounds in Exhall and Keresley in exchange for one cart out of two of fuel gathered in his woods in Coventry. From this Dugdale suggests that the land was once held by Leofric and Godiva.

The main landowners after the Earls of Chester were the Bottlers of Lancashire, who were succeeded by Julian Nethermill, an alderman of Coventry, who until the last war had a beautiful memorial in St Michael's church, Coventry. Julian's grandson, John Nethermill, sold the estate to Sir John Garrett, alderman of London. After that it passed to Sir Arthur Caley, then to William Cheslin.

Newland in Exhall was land granted to the monks of Coventry by Ranulf Blundeville, Earl of Chester. It took its name from the fact that it was new land acquired by the church. It was later deemed a manor containing a house and 270 acres of woodland, pasture and waste. In 1333 the land around the manor house was emparked and continued to be held by the monks of Coventry until the Dissolution in 1539.

Thereafter the house was held by Michael Camswell and the land known as Newland Park was granted by the Crown to John Wade and Thomas Gregory. In the reign of Elizabeth I the land and house passed into the hands of Stephen Hales, the brother of John Hales of New House, Keresley. Stephen died in 1574 and left it to his grandson, another Stephen. This Stephen moved his seat to Snitterfield and Newland Hall was left to fall into ruin. The grand fireplace, heavily carved and bearing the family armorials, was removed and re-erected in his brother Timothy's residence, Foleshill Hall, which stood in Lythalls Lane. In the mid-19th century it was moved to the home of Dr Phillips in Whitmore Park and is now lost. By the late 19th century all that remained of Newland Hall was a dried up moat, fishponds and Newland Hall Farm, which may have been constructed out of the remains of the hall. Monuments to the Hales family of Newland Hall can be found in the late 13th-century church of St Giles in Exhall.

The hall is said to have been the scene of an exorcism. A rich and avaricious individual haunted the scenes of his misdeeds and terrified the locals. Three exorcists were called in and lured the spirit into a bottle, sealed it and buried it in the rickyard. There it lay undisturbed for 100 years before it was accidentally unearthed. On being taken into the hall the bottle is said to have exploded in a cloud of smoke, which rushed up the chimney with loud rumblings. Thereafter noises were heard in that wall of the building, which was later demolished to end the haunting.

Moated Exhall Hall, also known as Hall Farm or Moat Farm, appears to date from the 18th

A 19th-century illustration showing the south-east prospect of St Giles, Exhall. Here were buried many of the Hales family of Newland Hall and Foleshill Hall.

century and is built upon the site of a more ancient building. Some have claimed it stands on the site of Aecca's hall, which is of course possible. In the late 18th and early 19th century it was a farmhouse occupied by Thomas Wale, a farmer from Weston, near Bulkington. Afterwards the farm was tenanted by Gabriel Barnett.

A real hero lies buried in the churchyard of St Giles, the old rector of Bedworth, the Revd Henry Bellairs. Before taking holy orders the reverend was a midshipman on HMS *Victory*. Bellairs fought at Trafalgar with Nelson and afterwards received a sword from King George III for his bravery. Afterwards he joined the army and is said to have just missed fighting at Waterloo. His family erected the lychgate at the entrance to the churchyard. The church itself contains burials of people not only from Exhall but also Newland and Whitmore Park.

It is said that the population increased when the canal was dug and a number of boatman's cottages were built on Bedworth Hill. The population increased again with the opening of Hawkesbury Colliery and many new cottages were built at the 'Waggon Overthrow' when Exhall

Colliery opened in around 1840. By 1883 the population numbered 881 persons. Children were educated in Bentley School, erected on part of the churchyard under the will of William Bentley in 1813.

The villagers used to hold a yearly wake called the 'Blackcurrant Wake', where the villagers marched to the church led by the Bedworth Brass Band, held a service then held events around the church and village. On the Sunday they ate blackcurrant pudding after dinner. On Wake Monday many women of the village visited the big houses and danced and sang. This was followed by a dinner of roast beef and plum pudding in Bentley School. The men gathered at the Bell Inn, which stood near the church, carried buckets of beer to the Bell Meadow and drank to their hearts' content.

In nearby Neale's Green in Rookery Lane from Keresley once stood Blackberry Hall, next to it once stood a large barrow-shaped mound, possibly prehistoric. Blackberry Hall is believed to have been an Elizabethan house, for inside on a beam was carved the date 1571. It was later the home of William Bentley, who endowed the school in Exhall. It is said that after he died the hall fell into ruin and was partly demolished. From the surviving section seven cottages were created. Several families of weavers moved into the cottages and in around 1825 Thomas Wale, who had previously run Moat Farm, Exhall, moved here. In 1925 it was said that only one of the cottages remained and of the hall all that survived was one of the original stones, which then served as a stand for a washtub.

Further Reading
Sir William Dugdale, *Warwickshire*, 1817 (revised).
Various newspaper cuttings, Local Studies.

FINHAM

Finham derives from two words, '*fina*' meaning woodpeckers and '*ham*' meaning a farmstead. It lies beyond Stivichall and Baginton, near to open countryside. The area has had some prehistoric activity, for in 1946 a Mr Woodhead discovered a small flint hand axe lying in the river by the golf course. As the axe was not badly water-stained it was believed to have been washed out of the gravel bank at a loop of the river. In the 1920s this same loop of river produced two quartzite and five flint implements. During work on the new sewage farm two flint arrowheads were found. Workmen digging a drain at King's Hill in 1938 unearthed a small crude pot. As it was found so deep down in undisturbed strata the object was sent to the British Museum and identified as a 'Pygmy Class' of vessel dating from between 1500 BC and 1000 BC.

Another fragment of the prehistoric landscape at Finham brought here by glacial movement is the Finham Boulder. In the 1930s archaeologist F.W. Shotton reported that the boulder was composed of Croft monzonite and, 'Like the Radford example, this had been used to cover the top of a well, and it now lies in a pool, at the side of the well. The farmer informs me that several horses were required to dislodge it a yard or so.' Shotton said the boulder, which lay in the farmyard of King Hill Farm, was on the crest of the hill, measured 5ft 6in and weighed over four tons. The boulder originated from a known site over 18 miles away and is thought to have been carried by an ice sheet coming from the northeast. Alternatively, it could have been moved by humans, making it and the hilltop well a sacred site.

The area was described as 'Finneham' in 1265; in 1284 the monks of Stoneleigh were given the area as a source of revenue. It was taken, with the abbey, by the Crown during the Dissolution and in 1550 it was sold to Thomas Kevett. In the 17th century it was described by Dugdale as a village 'that lyeth upon the back of the Sowe … In the past there were 12 houses there, but now only four remain.' In the same period it was acquired by the Bromleys of Baginton Hall who held it into the 19th century.

The area known as Hill or Kingshill, looking down on Finham, was known in the 13th century as Helenhulle, which changed in 1343 to Kynggeshill. This date of course discredits the old tale that says it takes it name from Charles I, who is said to have retreated from Coventry this way in 1642. The story may of course have a grain of truth and concern an earlier king. Alternatively the 'king' may refer to the boulder on the hill, as stones placed by prehistoric humans can be called 'king' stones.

The monks of Stoneleigh built a farming grange here which was sold after the Dissolution to Richard Andrews and Leonard Chamberlain of Woodstock, who sold it on in the same year to Thomas Gregory, whose family held it until the 19th century. In the 17th century the grange was surrounded by eight houses. The site has recently been built over.

Finham Green Farm in 1918.

In the early 20th century an article was written which describes a half-timbered house with a tall chimney, known as Pipe's Mill, in a wooded hollow flanked by a row of cottages. The building was all that remained of a once flourishing mill, used in early times as a flour mill, and later for manufacturing leather. The article states:

> *Mr Palmer, the present occupant of the house, told us that the leather making industry died out long before his time. The mill-house, he said, was once used by the monks of Stoneleigh Abbey as a resting place when they made their visits to Kenilworth and Baginton ... Traces of the mill dam still remain in the long grass by the riverside.*

Pipe's Mill, named after one of the owners, had a legend attached to it of an underground passage, which was reputed to lead to Stoneleigh Abbey. No trace of the supposed tunnel has ever been found. The writer continues:

> *Finham itself is a hamlet of Stoneleigh and is mainly associated now ... with the golf course and sewage works. True, there are few houses left today, and these are widely scattered, but the ancient and half-forgotten still holds its place against modernity. High up on a grassy open slope, stands a farmhouse [Kingshill Farm] with a history eight hundred years old ... Hill, as the house and its surrounds have been known since the twelfth century, was exhibited to us by Mr J.S.F. Cooper, who lives in the long, low, Elizabethan house, a house that 400 years ago replaced an ancient grange of the monks of Stoneleigh. It once bore the name of Kingshulle ...*
>
> *Mr Cooper and Mrs Cooper are eager to restore the house ... They are having beams uncovered, old furniture restored ... We were shown wonderful cupboards and dressers, oak doorways, and beams that have withstood four centuries of weather ... The stone foundations of the house are said to be the original masonry that supported the old monks grange. There is no doubt that an old well in the garden sixty feet deep and lined with stone all the way down, dates from the time of the grange. The water, incidentally, is a pure as any in the county.*

Our writer, the anonymous, 'R.J.M.', goes on to mention a local character called Tommy Timms, known affectionately as the 'Stoneleigh Landmark.' Mr Cooper recalled that Tommy lived in one of the cottages at Pipe's Mill and would never work if it rained. When he did work he would constantly beg for a 'mashin' o' tea.' When he needed a new coat or hat he would exchange with a scarecrow.

As R.J.M. stated, Finham is remembered now as then for the sewage works and the golf course. The sewage works were brought into operation in 1932, using the bacteria-bed system. Coventry Golf Club, which runs onto the boundary of Baginton, was opened on 9 May 1912 by golfing greats Harry Vardon and James Braid, both British Open Champions. Hugh Rotherham of Keresley Grange was a member of the club and it was he who invented the term 'bogey' which is now a standard golfing term.

Further Reading
Coventry Family History Journal, September 2002.
Coventry Standard and various news cuttings, Local Studies.

FLETCHAMSTEAD

Fletchamstead lies between Canley and Tile Hill and consisted of two small hamlets known as Over and Nether Fletchamstead, spelt in 1185 as 'Flighamstead'. The name is thought to originate from the Old English '*flicce*', a flitch of bacon, and '*stede*', said to refer to the produce of a farm. Henry I (1110–1135) granted land to Gerard the Hermit and between 1149 and 1161 a chapel and then a watermill were built. The churchyard was said to have been consecrated by Walter Durent, Bishop of Coventry. Both these buildings and much of the land were owned by the Knights Templar. A stone coffin from the chapel later found its way into Duggins Lane, Tile Hill, where it was used as a cattle-trough. After the suppression of the Templars in 1314 the land and property came into the hands of the Knights Hospitaller. By 1487 the buildings and land were owned by Coventry lawyer John Smith.

Sir William Dugdale recorded that in the 17th century the area was split in two halves, Over and Nether Fletchamstead. The main village was Over Fletchamstead (off the present Torrington Avenue), which consisted of Over Fletchamstead Hall and 31 cottages. Nether Fletchamstead (behind Queen Margaret's Road, Canley) consisted of one cottage and another smaller hall called Nether Fletchamstead Hall. A park containing deer surrounded the smaller Nether Fletchamstead Hall. The 'park' in Park Wood and Cannon Park, Canley comes from this long-gone deer park.

As Fletchamstead lay on the Stoneleigh Estate Sir Thomas Leigh, son of Sir Thomas and Lady Alicia Leigh, who first acquired the estate, built Over Fletchamstead Hall and park. Tradition states

An early 19th-century painting of Nether Fletchamstead Hall. (CCL)

that Charles I once stayed at the hall, although this could be confused with his stay at Stoneleigh Abbey. Members of the Leigh family lived at Over Fletchamstead Hall until the 17th century when it became the residence of Thomas Flynt of Allesley. This hall is said to have been demolished in the early 19th century and another built on the site. Nether Fletchamstead Hall was acquired during the reign of Henry VII by John Smyth, an attorney, living in Spon Street. His son Henry succeeded him and in 1497 laid out the deer park and improved the hall. In 1690 the Leighs acquired the manor from one of the Smyths of Crabbet in Sussex, but it does not appear to have been occupied in the 19th century. In 1817 there were only seven houses standing in the area now simply called Fletchamstead.

Mary Dormer Harris visited the hall in the 1930s and wrote that she:

> ... went along the grass-grown ways, and into the little gate under the immense dark yew. It was all very still, save for the riot of birds in the neglected garden. I think I would find no-one, and indeed no-one answered ... Peeping in the curtainless window, I saw the bare room, where my cousin's harp used to stand, and on the other side of the door where my uncle used to read prayers after breakfast in his dear husky voice ... In the evening when the lamp was lit, and the women folk had brought out their sewing, he would also read out aloud from some improving book.
>
> Even now I associate his memory with the scent of flowers. He would gather jasmine for you from the tree, which grew up by the side of the door. Evening scented stock was sown in the garden; and year by year the evening primrose came up...I have written before of my uncle James Harris, who passed his whole life here, of his gentleness, his love for children, the mild radiancy of his cherubic face which no sorrow could dim, of his everlasting goodness to men and animals whose working days were well nigh done. Now I seem to see that fate that dealt so hardly with him...giving him neither wife nor child and taking away wealth and health...

Further Reading

Coventry Family History Society Journal, No.7, September 2002.
Mary Dormer Harris, *Some Manors, Churches and Villages of Warwickshire*, 1937.
Sir William Dugdale, *Warwickshire*, 1817 (revised).

FOLESHILL

The name Foleshill comes from 'Folkeshull', meaning 'the people's meeting place on the hill'. Many years ago a large sandstone rock known locally as the 'Donkey Stone' stood on a grass verge in Little Heath on the corner of the present Foleshill Road and Old Church Road. Unable to explain its presence here, a legend grew up among locals to explain it: when Foleshill Church was being built the stone was brought here by donkey cart from Corley Rocks; one stone fell off and was never picked up. The Donkey Stone was of unknown size, but apparently big enough to prevent anyone moving it. I suspect that in fact the Donkey Stone had prehistoric or Roman origins.

It has been suspected for some time that the Foleshill Road is of great age, possibly Roman. It would follow the line of a suspected Roman road from Mancetter, through Bedworth, Longford and Coventry to Baginton and beyond. All of these places have place-names associated with Roman passage and have turned up Roman finds. Foleshill is no different, for on 14 January 1793 the *Coventry Mercury* reported:

> On the 17th of December last, was discovered in a meadow at Foleshill, belonging to Mr. Jos. Whiting, of that place, in digging a trench, about two feet below the surface, an earthen pot, containing upwards of 1800 Roman copper coins, principally of the Emperors Constantine, Constans, Constantius and Magnentius; most of which remain in the possession of Mr Whiting for the inspection of the curious. And on Saturday last, in continuing the same trench, he found another earthen jar, containing a great quantity of larger coin; but the latter are in greater preservation.

The Stoney Stanton Road may also be ancient. Originally called the Sewell Pavement it may have originally run towards Wolvey and beyond.

A new bridge being built on the Manor Farm Estate, Bell Green, in 1950. (CCL)

71

The post office in Bell Green in around 1905. (CCL)

The Domesday Survey of 1086 records that Godiva held Ansty and Foleshill in the Knightlow, also known as the 'Bumbelowe' Hundred, and there was enough land for 21 ploughs. The land was occupied by 30 villeins, six boarders and two slaves. There was also woodland one league square. The Norman Nicholas held the lands of the Saxon Countess Godgifu, 'at farm from the King.' How these were divided between Ansty and Foleshill is not known.

The hill of the people referred to in the place-name must have been a Saxon moot mound, where locals would assemble for the *'folcgemot'*, the folk moot. The site of this mound is not known, but it may have been near the original Saxon village centre, in the present Old Church Road around the chapel of St Laurence, said to have been founded by Earl Leofric and later given to Coventry Priory, although some sources suggest the original settlement was at Hall Green. A known meeting place called the Wolfpitelideyate (the hollow way to the wolf pit) stood near the boundary of Exhall at Rowleys Green. This possible moot mound appears to take its name from a wolfpit, a pit for catching wolves. Another later meeting place where justice was meted out was probably at Courthouse Green, the site of the mediaeval courthouse, later Courthouse Farm.

The lordship passed to the earls of Chester and the Montalts, who gave over the chapel and some land to

Looking down Bell Green Road in the 1930s. (CCL)

Foleshill Hall in Lythalls Lane, as it appeared around 1800.

the priory. The principal tenant in the 13th century was Vitalis de Foleshill, then his son of the same name. It then passed through various hands including Arnold de Bois, William la Zouch and the Greens. After the Dissolution the priory's lands passed to the Crown and a number of small freehold farms were created, such as the 'Beechwaste' granted to Michael Cameswell in 1544.

Beyond the wastes were the districts of Tackley (later Hawkesbury) and Henley. These probably originated as woodland settlements separate from Foleshill village, as John de Nuweres was known as Lord of Tackley in 1368. By the 17th century the lost settlement of Tackley only existed as a small group of fields named Tackley Grounds. Henley was first mentioned in 1359 when Sir Robert Gresley and his wife granted the manor to Sir Balwin and his wife Dame Ida. It was then passed to the Ferevilles and at some time appears to have been depopulated, leaving only Henley Mill. The mill itself lay on land belonging to Coventry Priory and in the 14th century was occupied by Walter the Miller. This mill in its various guises lasted into the 20th century, although it ceased operation in the 1880s.

In 1587 the entire manor of Foleshill was held by William Willoughby until it passed out of the family's hands in 1629. The estate was then held by the Hopkins family until 1799 when it passed to Richard Northey (a nephew) who assumed the named Hopkins Northey. Later it passed through marriage to George Ives Irby, 4th Lord Boston, who died in 1935. It was then run by his trustees.

Foleshill consists of many distinct communities: Bell Green, Courthouse Green, Alderman's Green, Rowley's Green, Ash Green, Woodshires Green, Hall Green, Edgewick, Tackley, Longford, Holbrooks, Great Heath, Little Heath, Paradise and Penny Park.

The Manor House of Foleshill is a problem, as one would expect it to have been within a short distance of the original village centre. What was known as Foleshill Hall stood opposite Foleshill

Foleshill village centre, with the church of St Laurence, photographed in the late 19th century.

A late 19th century drawing of Foleshill Hall in Lythalls Lane. (CCL)

Hall Farm in Lythalls Lane. It became a public house called the Foleshill Olde Hall in 1915. The oldest part of the building dated to about 1700, but it is said that a drawing from 1883 suggested that the west side of the hall was considerably older. When the hall was refurbished the staircase, said to date from the early 17th century, was reused. The old hall was recently pulled down during the building of a new bypass.

In the district of Hall Green (called le Hallegrene in 1411), between Hall Green Road and the Tackford Brook (near the present Sycamore Road), stood a building called the Manor House. This was later referred to as Manor House Farm; the age of this building, which disappeared in 1955 under the new housing estate, is unknown and it may well be the original Foleshill Hall, home of Timothy Hales in the late 16th century. It has been suggested that Hall Green was the original settlement in the area on the main thoroughfare. Foleshill's more isolated church, which lies in Foleshill (Church End), appears to date from the 14th century. It does however contain a Norman font and when it was restored in 1889 it was said that Saxon or Norman remains of the earlier building were found. Was the original village at Hall Green and the 'folkshulle' the moot mound from which the parish takes its name on or near the present church? Was there a chapel associated with the moot mound or was Church End (which bears the name Foleshill) the original settlement, possibly depopulated by plague and moved to Hall Green? The fact that the church is said to have been built in 1360 and the City Annals record a 'great pestilence' in 1368, coupled with the fact that the oldest reference to Hall Green is in 1411 may be significant. That said it has been suggested that the

Children photographed in 1890 looking into Springfield Brook in open countryside at the bottom of Eagle Street. The area is now completely built upon and the brook is culverted. (CCL)

Foleshill Road, photographed in 1910. This was the first tramway track laid in Coventry. (CCL.)

original settlement was at Little Heath, which like much of the rest of Foleshill existed as a small settlement in an area of open heath land.

From the 13th to the 19th century there were incursions onto the heath and woodland of Foleshill. Up until the Dissolution parts held by the priory and by the manor of Cheylesmore were slowly being converted into common fields, farmland, small homesteads and large estate farms. The first estate mentioned in Foleshill is a house with farmland, meadow and pasture held by Arnold de Bois in 1277. The same estate is described in 1299 as consisting of a house, mill, woodland, farmland and nine tenants, with six houses. This must be Hall Green.

The same mill, known as Foleshill Mill, was still in use in the 1950s. It was at that time run by Mr F. Faulconbridge, who was brought to the mill by his father Issac in 1883. The family lived in the Mill House, which stood next to the watermill, a three-storey brick building with a Georgian façade. The building was probably much older, for it contained ancient oak ceiling beams, heavily carved 17th-century window shutters, a ceiling canopy, oak staircase and stone fireplace. During the 19th century Joseph Galloway of Grange Farm, Longford, was the miller, followed by the Eld family who sold flour and delivered bread on a horse-drawn cart as far as Rugby. Trade flagged but was revived by the Faulconbridges who also supplied the power to drive 30 looms for the Wests in the adjoining cottages. A short distance from Foleshill Mill stood the windmill from which Windmill Lane takes its name.

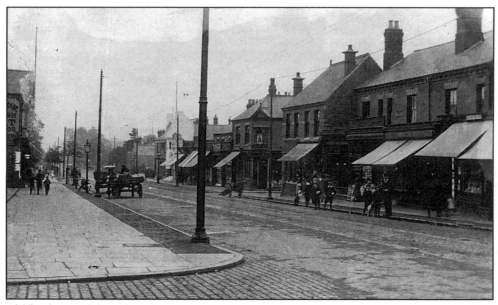

Foleshill Road in 1910, looking south from the corner of Station Street. (CCL)

By the 15th century Foleshill had become more and more enclosed. Many smallholdings were eventually swallowed up by larger family estates such as those owned by the Holbrooks and Greens. In 1776 the Hopkins family had a 413-acre estate that they let out to three farms. Another estate, known as the Foleshill Hall Estate, was owned by a Willenhall man in 1839 and farmed as a single 165-acre farm by Edward Lythall, a name that is remembered in Lythalls Lane. In the Tithe Award of 1841 the area is shown to have 104 owners, and although much of it was enclosed some common and heath land remained.

Apart from agriculture the area was once dug for coal. In 1579 Christopher Wynold was licensed to dig a pit and prospect for coal in what is now Black Horse Road. By 1622 four more men were prospecting successfully for coal. During the 17th and 18th century surface mines were created in Tackley, Sydnall, Hawkesbury, Little Heath, Longford and Bell Green. The Parrott family of Hawkesbury Hall invested heavily in the coal business from at least 1721. Later, as part of Parrott, Ferneyhough and Wieldon of Hawkesbury Colliery, they invested in the creation of the Oxford and Coventry canals to carry coal out of the area. It is said that the people of Foleshill lined the canal banks to see the first coal barges travelling to Coventry. From strong beginnings the collieries in these areas went into decline with only 30 coal miners left in the parish in 1831. By the late 19th century only Hawkesbury Colliery and the Victoria Colliery survived. Victoria eventually closed in 1870 because of fires.

Mining increased the population of the area. People lived mainly in half-timbered and mud roadside cottages. The Compton Census of 1676 states that there were 284 adults and Dugdale's *Warwickshire* records that in 1730 there were 20 houses at Great Heath, 11 at Little Heath, 12 in

Courtaulds chimney in Foleshill was once the tallest in the land, measuring 365ft. (CCL)

Court House Farm, incorporating the Courthouse from which the district took its name. (CCL)

Holbrooks, 21 in Sydnall, 5 in Coney Lane (Grange Road, Longford), 19 in Rowley's Green, 20 in Longford, 19 in Hall Green and 22 in Bell Green. Courthouse Green, Alderman's Green and Foxford are not mentioned but may be included in the last entry.

In the 18th century weaving also spread into the area, bringing a further increase in population. By 1801 it was 3,026, with 600 inhabited houses. There were 937 weavers in the district. By 1818 this had risen to 2,544 weavers working 1,732 looms, mostly by hand. Power looms were soon added and the once well-known 'top-shop' was created.

It is interesting that with this large population of workers, Foleshillites appear to have given huge support to trade unionism. The *Coventry Herald & Observer* of 28 March 1834 reports an extraordinary funeral:

> *On Tuesday last the funeral of Mr Pearson took place, in the burying ground of the Independent Chapel, Foleshill. The deceased was a leading member of the Trades Union, and was buried with a ceremony peculiar to the Order. The procession consisted of about fifteen hundred persons, partly women who were arrayed in white and wearing hoods. A number of men, who we understand to be officers of the Union, were dressed in gowns. By one of these was carried the Bible on a cushion, the Wardens carrying battle-axes, made of wood, and the Tylers their drawn swords ... The funeral excited considerable interest, and was witnessed by several thousand spectators.*

The population of Foleshill during the 19th century remained fairly constant, with many people resident in the area working or owning businesses in Coventry. Among the houses were the odd gentleman's residences such as Bird Grove (named after the abundance of birds and trees) a semi-detached house, half of which still survives in George Eliot Road. Houses such as this were still in a

A 19th-century drawing of the bridge on Alderman's Green Road just below Foleshill Mill. (CCL)

Open-topped trams picking up the girls who worked at Courtaulds in around 1910.

semi-rural position and in 1841 Bird Grove became the home of Robert Evans and his impressionable daughter Mary Ann, later known to the world as George Eliot. In the other side of the house (now gone) lived ribbon manufacturer Abijah Pears and his wife Elizabeth (sister of Charles Bray), who introduced Mary Ann to Charles and Cara Bray of Rosehill, Radford, an event which was to change the course of her life. Here in semi-rural Foleshill George Eliot began her writing career. The area later became part of Bishopsgate Green, which in 1851 consisted solely of a small cluster of buildings in the bend of the Coventry Canal off the Foleshill or Leicester Road.

The weaving trade in Coventry and Foleshill plunged into decline from 1860, when the weavers went on strike. Foreign ribbons flooded the market and many went hungry and emigrated. In 1861 there were 8,140 souls in the parish, 6,429 of whom worked in the ribbon trade. No records tell of the initial impact but by 1871 the population had decreased by nearly 2,000. However, this was not the end of weaving. In 1882 W.H. Grant's Livingstone Silk Mill opened in Lockhurst Lane, producing a variety of items, including silk pictures like 'Stevengraphs'. It was still there in 1937 weaving ribbons, club badges, name-tags and labels. During the early 20th century other silk weaving factories were set up and in 1904 Courtaulds set up their first rayon factory on the Foleshill Road. Later they set up a separate branch of the factory at Little Heath.

Survivals in the hand-weaving trade could also still be found in Foleshill in the 20th century. In the *Coventry Standard* in 1927, a reporter wrote:

> *Walking along a quiet Foleshill lane the other day in a thoughtful mood my reverie was suddenly broken by the click clack of a loom, a sound which used to be so familiar years ago, but which is rather a novelty today. I looked in the direction from which came the noise and saw a sweet-faced grey-haired old lady sitting at a handloom. There was a small cushion against the breast piece, and this she leaned against as she cast the shuttle from side to side, all unconscious of the fact that I was watching her.*
>
> *The door stood partly open, I knocked and walked in … and sitting on a small stool was a white haired man busy filling quills for his wife's shuttle. I said 'Good morning, I understood there was no hand-loom weaving done now,' to which the man replied, 'I see that man Spectator in Warwickshire, says so in the Coventry Standard, but that loom you see there has been running for more than 70 years, and across the way there is a factory with four hand-looms running in it.'*

Bird Grove, home of George Eliot and her father until his death.

The old lady said that her father ran the loom before her and she showed him a silk scarf her father made on the loom 60 years previously. She screwed it up tightly in her hand and stretched it out again, showing that the treatment had failed to crease

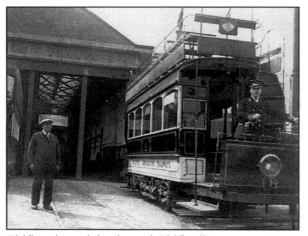

Foleshill tram depot was built on the site of the Foleshill Workhouse.

the scarf. The writer continued, 'In an apologetic sort of tone the old lady told me that having to do her domestic duties she can only weave about sixteen yards of material per week.'

During the 20th century many engineering firms, among others, set up in Foleshill. The most noted was Alfred Herbert's at Edgewick, which for a time was the largest machine tool company in the world. As houses were built along the lanes in the separate communities they eventually all joined together to create the present urban sprawl.

Apart from the old church of St Laurence, Foleshill had no other church until 1759 when the Baptists built a chapel at Longford, followed by the Foleshill Independents in 1795. John Wesley is said to have visited Foleshill in 1779 and by 1791 14 of his followers were meeting at Hall Green. In 1809 the Hall Green group met in a weavers workshop and in 1813 opened a chapel in Bell Green. In 1832 a chapel was opened in Lockhurst Lane. St Paul's church was opened in 1842 and was attended by Mary Ann Evans (George Eliot) and her father, who was a plate-bearer. It was while attending this church and Holy Trinity in the city centre that the future novelist first changed her faith, later refusing to attend.

Foleshill claims to have been the site of the oldest Co-operative Society in England. A society was formed in 1832 in Lockhurst Lane, 12 years before the Rochdale pioneers and the Coventry Society. The first trams to serve Coventry went along the Foleshill Road to Bedworth. One Foleshillite wrote of the introduction of steam trams in 1884: 'This was I suppose the greatest ever event seen in Foleshill up to that time. All Foleshillites were out lining the route as this 'iron horse' came jogging along, blowing out smoke, for it was fed with coal like a locomotive.' Trams, later electrified, became a common sight along the Foleshill Road and Stoney Stanton Road from 1899, and a main depot was built in the district, on the Foleshill Road near the junction with Old Church Road, the site of the present fire station.

A writer in the *Coventry Standard* in 1960 wrote:

It is difficult to reconcile the Foleshill of today with the place 70 years ago. The church of St Paul was set in the midst of meadows and cornfields, presented a rural and picturesque scene. Tall trees lined either side of the Foleshill Road from the General Wolfe (then only a cottage) to the Partings of the Heath ... Old and familiar walks have disappeared such as Edgewick Fields (now Cross Road) where farmer Sidwell and family abode. Also Massers Fields linking Lythalls Lane to Holbrook Lane, and the Black Pad from Lockhurst Lane to Halford Lane in Keresley.

Posing by a tram on the Bell Green Road at Courthouse Green in the 1930s. Beyond can be seen the dip in the road as its approaches Bell Green.

Beautiful birds nested in the hedgerows, such as all varieties of finches and the yellow hammer, in addition to the thrushes and blackbirds, the lark and nightingale and the little wrens. The corncrake could often be heard from the main in harvest time and the peewit in the spring.

Within this lovely scene Foleshillites played sports, forming clubs such as the Foleshill Albions and Foleshill St Paul's Cricket Club. The Foleshill Lilywhite fête was held in 1901, in a field adjoining the Angel Hotel. The main attraction of the day was a cricket match played by local gents wearing top hats, frock coats, flannels, white shirts and black ties. One player was the notable Dr John Orton, who treated patients across the north of Coventry and was noted for driving his horse and gig along the canal when it was frozen.

The General Wolfe, previously a cottage pub, is interesting because the inn was in existence as early as 1838, and the parish of Foleshill had a reputation. The *Coventry Herald & Observer* reported on 28 September of that year that:

The late 19th-century General Woolfe pub on the Foleshill Road in around 1910. This replaced the earlier country cottage inn favoured by local farmers.

The Prince William Henry on the Foleshill Road next to the Coventry Canal. It was under the land lordship of William Arnett in around 1900.

On Thursday night last week, a man named Cooper, on his way to Coventry, called at the General Wolfe Public House, Foleshill, where he fell in company with some ruffians with which that parish abounds, who, after snaring him by some false directions as to his road, followed him out, waylaid him, and robbed him of two watches and nineteen shillings in money. At present we believe, they are not detected.

Unveiling a temporary plaster war memorial at the junction of Holbrook Lane and Durbar Avenue in 1919. A bronze copy was never made. Foleshill station is in the background. (CCL)

Tusses Bridge in around 1910, crossing the canal on the Hawkesbury Lane. The pub by the bridge is the Elephant and Castle. (CCL)

The *Herald* later adds that they sent him down Carpenters Lane in Lockyers Lane and robbed him. Lockyers Lane is now Lockhurst Lane. It takes its name from land belonging to Anketil Locard in the 12th century. Locard may have taken his own name from an area abutting Whitmore Park, in 1335 still known as Lockearsmore.

At the bottom of Lockhurst Lane, taking up that corner on the Foleshill Road, once stood a small area called Vauxhall. Vauxhall House and its gardens were built in the 18th century by a churchwarden

A rare view of the waterfall below Foleshill Mill in around 1906. For scale note the man standing above.

of Holy Trinity and a grocer called Hill. It took its name from Vauxhall Pleasure Gardens in London. When the new burial ground was opened Hill removed a large number of burial stones from the old one and used them as flagstones for the floor of the house and garden. This Vauxhall may have also been a pleasure garden; it was the home of the Baker family around the turn of the 20th century and lay derelict by the late 1930s.

Opposite the house of Tony Guy on the Foleshill Road lies a row of blue bricks and a grassed area, all that remains of Chapel Square, a collection of cottages built in around 1850. Lily Gallagher was born at No.19 Chapel Square in 1907. In 1987 she wrote down some memories:

> I was one of six children, my father was a miner. We were all poor down the square, but happy, clean and well fed. Our house was two up one down; some had three bedrooms and a little front room. I always remember the gas mantle and the little grey cooker, there were no water toilets, we all had to share buckets with a wooden seat. We had to carry the water from the tap half-way down the square.

Lily remembered that Monday was washday:

> It was lovely to see all the white washing on the line, the smell was lovely and on washday all the cobbles were washed with the soapy water. Every year we had a carnival around the square and a party ... All the gardens were in front of the houses, all kept very neat and tidy, but they were never separated by fences, no-one ever cut through anyone else's garden.
>
> I remember before Courtaulds was built it was just fields, I believe R. Whites pop people owned it and we used to go there to play. The Three Horse Shoes has been rebuilt ... farther up was a big old house in its own grounds ... we never went up the drive because we were frightened my Mum used to say it was a workhouse and we would go there if we weren't good ... Then there was the tram depot, which I think is the fire station.
>
> Every night at the same time six trams (or more), no tops on, came out to fetch the Courtaulds girls at Lockhurst Lane, when they finished work at 5.30. Mrs Cashmore lived at number one Chapel Square and she had a small bay window that looked over the Foleshill Road, which she used as a little general store in which she sold everything. At the side of her shop she had a shed affair in which she cooked fish and chips and they were lovely, you had a big paper full of scallops for one penny.

The workhouse, or Foleshill House of Industry, was built in the late 18th century and dealt with the poor of the parish. Foleshill was a particularly large parish and within the county of the city of Coventry. Here inmates were put to work producing saleable material to help pay for their keep.

Further Reading
Gordon Cowley, *Folks Hill*.
David McGrory, *City of Coventry: Images from the Past*, 1996.
Various newspapers, Local Studies.

GOSFORD GREEN

When one thinks of Gosford Green today one imagines a large triangle of grass between Walsgrave and Binley roads. However, historically it ran up to Stoke Knob and across towards Jabet's Ash, Shortley and the Charterhouse. The old Folly Lane, renamed Humber Road in the 20th century, was an ancient back way into Coventry, the upper section of which crossed Gosford Green. The name means 'the green above the goose ford'.

At the extreme west of the green once stood a hermitage and chapel dedicated to St Margaret. This chapel was first mentioned in an agreement dated July 1456 between the prior and the vicar of Holy Trinity, when it was referred to as being newly erected. After the Dissolution the chapel fell into disuse and was converted into a tithe barn, within a small enclosure at the top of Far Gosford Street. In 1647 it was referred to as 'the tithe barne', giving a yearly income to Trinity Church of £1 13s 4d. T.W. Whitley wrote of it before its destruction to make way for the green in the late 19th century:

It was of considerable size, much out of repair, and its roof let in the wind and rain. At times it was occupied by itinerant players, who visited the town ... [and] would perform some piece of horror, dread and treachery, which would invariably draw a miscellaneous audience, most of the juvenile class, who for their pennies expended

Syd Squire's 'Chair-O-Planes' on Gosford Green in June 1947.

received from the woe bespoken tragedians, dressed in soiled and bespattered costumes, an amount of rant and raving. There was a large beam of the roof of the barn … near the stage end, upon which a number of youths usually perched like so many crows … One piece often acted without scenery was 'Maria Martin' [murder in the Red Barn] *and a friend who remembers a performance there relates how he saw a duel to the death, in which the villain of the piece got killed, and a few minutes after got up and exclaimed, 'Hallady, I'm wounded,' to which Halladay replied, 'Mortally, I fear me Lord,' when his Lordship gave a sigh, shouted, 'Take this to my Lady,' then danced a double shuffle, fell on the boards and died a second time.*

A real fight to the death nearly took place on the green on 17 September 1398, St Lambert's Day, when Thomas Mowbray, Duke of Norfolk, met Henry Bolingbroke, Duke of Hereford, in a non-event that would change the course of English history. Bolingbroke had accused Mowbray of treason, and during an inquest accused him of murdering his uncle. Mowbray denied the charges and Parliament resolved that the two men should settle the matter in single combat. The event was heralded throughout the land. Mowbray had a new suit of armour constructed in Milan, while Bolingbroke had his created by the best German armourers.

As thousands flocked to Coventry to watch, Mowbray waited at the family home, Caludon Castle, while Bolingbroke stayed with Sir Henry Bagot at Baginton Castle. Richard II camped with the royal army of 10,000 knights and 20,000 archers and foot-soldiers near the Ball Hill end of the green, which thereafter was called King's Field. On the day itself squires helped Mowbray into his armour in a tent, while Bolingbroke dressed in a stone tower nearby.

Bolingbroke awaited the fight astride his white horse, covered in blue and green velvet, embroided with silver antelopes and swans. Asked aloud why he was there, he replied, 'I am Henry of Lancaster, Duke of Hereford. I have come here to do my endeavour against Thomas Mowbray, Duke of Norfolk, as a traitor, untrue to God, the king, his realm and me.' He then took out his sword, held it before him and swore that his quarrel was just, before dismounting and sitting upon a great chair draped in green velvet.

King Richard then entered with all the peers of the realm and they took their seats upon a great dais erected for the event. Thomas Mowbray, Duke of Norfolk, then swearing his cause was also true said aloud 'God aid him that hath the right.'

As both men were seated their lances were checked and returned to them. Both quickly mounted their horses. As the trumpet blew Bolingbroke was already thundering towards his challenger. Mowbray had just started kicking his horse forward when the royal heralds ran on shouting, 'Ho! Ho!'

Bolingbroke reined in his horse, while Mowbray stumbled to a sudden halt and both men were surrounded by soldiers and called to yield their weapons, which they did. They were told to retake their seats while the king and council deliberated. Two hours later the heralds called the vast crowd to silence while Sir John Bushy read aloud their decision. He stated that Bolingbroke had 15 days to leave the realm and never return for 10 years, unless ordered by the king, on pain of death. Mowbray, because he had sown 'sedition in the realm by his words' was ordered to leave the realm forever. All

The granite memorial erected on Gosford Green to commemorate the duel between Bolingbroke and Mowbray.

his estates were confiscated and he would receive a yearly allowance of £1,000. Bolingbroke also had his estates confiscated and was given £2,000 a year.

Both men then had to appear before the king and swear that they would not continue the argument abroad. The king and his army left the city, Mowbray left for Venice where it is said he died of melancholy, and Bolingbroke, who was one of the nation's favourites, was said to have been seen off by a crowd of 40,000.

During his exile Henry Bolingbroke's father, John of Gaunt, convinced the king to reduce his son's punishment. All would probably have been well, but in 1399 John of Gaunt died and Richard took over his vast estates. Henry returned to England and demanded the return of the Lancastrian estates. He then decided to claim the throne itself through his descent from Henry III and within months Richard II was dead, murdered by Henry's order, and Bolingbroke had become Henry IV. A commemorative stone to mark the event which led to Bolingbroke's exile, which was written about in Shakespeare's *Richard II*, still stands on what little remains of the green.

The green was also the scene of another unusual event in 1469. Earl Rivers and his son, father and brother of Elizabeth Woodville, queen of Edward IV, were beheaded on the green by order of the Earl of Warwick, who had secretly led an uprising in Yorkshire. Later still on two occasions the army of Edward IV waited on this open area while demands were made at Gosford gate for the Earl of Warwick to leave the city to fight.

Alderman Andrews wrote of the green in 1891:

> When I went to reside at Gosford Green in 1863 its surface was extremely unlevelled, and did not appear fit for a fight between knights . . . subsequent investigation showed that the natural surface of the ground had never been disturbed, except by abortive draining operations. The ground was undulated in a series of hills and hollows a few feet high or deep, the only level spot being a patch of about half an acre, at the lowest point, nearly in the middle of the Green.

Andrews also tells us that the highest point was at the Swan Lane end, where there was a hillock about three feet high. Nearby was a large depression about four feet deep, which flooded in winter and earned the nickname the 'Old Slough.' At the tip of the green was a circular enclosure called 'Tithe Barn Piece' which until 1880 was a nursery for ornamental shrubs and fruit trees. East of this stood a four-foot high mound, a regular vantage point for watching the cricket played on the green. This later turned out to be a late mediaeval dump containing 10 waggonloads of red tiles, floor tiles, rough pottery, iron dross, oyster shells and tons of bones.

In November 1882 the council recommended the purchase of Tithe Barn Piece from Holy Trinity Church to add it to the green, which they proposed to enlarge and improve into a recreational ground. Work started on levelling the green in 1884 and was continued during the winter of 1885–6 by unemployed weavers. It is said that 150 loads of earth full of bones were taken from St Michael's churchyard to level the stretch along the Binley Road and grass grew particularly well there. Work was finally finished in 1889.

Further Reading
David McGrory, *History of Coventry*, 2003.
Eric Bramwell, *Coventry Cameos*, 1977.
Newspapers and cuttings, Local studies.

HILLFIELDS
(ALSO KNOWN AS HARNALL)

The name means, obviously, 'the fields on the hill'. Harnall comes from the Old English '*haran heale*,' meaning 'the land at the boundary', referring to the boundaries of priory land. Of the ancient history of Hillfields nothing is known, except that on top of Primrose Hill there once stood a long mound called the 'Giant's Grave.' Mounds which bear such titles are usually prehistoric burial mounds. Folklore remembers that they are graves, but for centuries they were assumed to be the graves of giants because of their size.

The first mention of a road through Harnall was in 1170 when most of district belonged to Coventry Priory. In 1279, when it consisted of six cottages and a number of crofts, parts were also held by Roger de Montalt. Five men were tenants of Roger, and each of them had a tenant of their own. Some of these also had under-tenants. By 1411 the priory held a major part of the manor alone and in the demesne had a house or grange, which may have stood on the site of Primrose Hill House.

Another landowner until the Dissolution was the Hospital of St John. That estate consisted of a mansion or grange, 13 fields and Harnale or Swanswell Pool. After the Dissolution the estate came to John Hales and the priory's land was granted to the Corporation. Much of the district lay in an area anciently called Hasilwood, meaning 'the hazel wood', and the northern part consisted of wasteland in the 14th century. Also at that time there is mention of Priors Harnall, near Swan's Lane, and Potters Harnall in the north going into Stoke. It is likely that these were hamlets.

Primrose Hill Park before World War One. The large mound on the right is probably the 'Giant's Grave'. (CCL)

Original Victorian houses built at the time of the creation of the Hillfields district. Here we see Primrose Hill Street in the 1960s.

In the 19th century Hillfields as we know it did not exist. The lower section of Harnall around the Swanswell Fields was described as 'rich with waving corn, and had two pools of water of much greater area than the present pond [Swanswell], and that portion around the pools which was not cultivated, formed a rank and secluded marsh where wildfowl sported amongst the tall reeds and rushes.'

The low ground around the pools was the home to widgeon, moorhens and dippers, now rare in Warwickshire. In the reeds were warblers and the pools were said to be teeming with fish: pike, perch, roach, tench and eels, giving good sport to anglers up to the 1960s.

It was a 'a wild and weird place. The water was bordered by fine old pollard willows ... and the ground gradually rose from the edge of the water into Hillfields.' Looking down the view of the pool was almost obstructed by the many oaks, elms, chestnuts and maples that surrounded it and near the pool by the present Wheatley Street bus station stood an ancient stone mansion called Swanswell House, believed locally to have been the country house of the Bishop of

Crowds heading for Highfield Road for the football in the 1930s. Three or four trams were also used to ferry supporters to the ground.

Coventry. As the bishop already had a residence near the priory it is likely that the house was merely owned by the priory.

The open agricultural land that was to become Hillfields originally held just a farm, one or two cottages and Primrose Hill House, first mentioned in 1753 but thought to be on the site of the early monastic grange. The prior's quarry, dug by monks, is recorded as being adjacent to it before 1224. The site presently lies behind Coronation Road. There was also a windmill, which stood at the bottom of a dirt track in open countryside. Its former site now lies between the Coventry and Warwickshire Hospital and Lincoln Street. The windmill, which stood in the Windmill Field near Bishopsgate Green, was already 'old' in 1851.

Joseph Gutteridge wrote of Hillfields in the 19th century:

The highest part of Hillfields is called Primrose Hill, from which a path runs across two fields into Swan Lane. This hill is beautifully wooded ... one part of the hill had been quarried extensively and to a great depth [for the city walls] ... In the deep holes made by the excavations forest trees now grow, towering by straight stems to a height of thirty or forty feet, their heads ... almost impenetrable to the sun's rays. It well deserved the name it bore for in my early recollection it was a mass of primroses and daffodils.

Of Primrose Hill House he recalled that the mansion was set among beautiful trees, oaks, elms, maple and firs, home of nightingales and many rare migratory birds. The spot, he recalls, 'most beautiful in summer time, when enlivened by the songs of birds that swarmed thither, will never be forgotten.'

A list of historic events composed in 1849 tells us that in 1828:

... the fields lying between Swanswell-pool and Primrose Hill began to be converted into building land. The first house erected in Hill-Fields, or as it is now called, 'New

Town', is situate in King William-street, a row of houses adjoining the field in Harnal-lane, having been reared a short time before. There are now about 6,000 inhabitants in the district.

These inhabitants were mainly weavers and watchmakers.

Victorian historian T.W. Whitley described the area:

In 1830 Paynes-lane was only a minor road, barely passable and a fordrift or cart-road stretched therefrom to Harnall-brook towards the town, where East-street now stands, whilst the new streets on Spittlemoor were not laid out. A few houses existed in East-street, which not being made, its surface was in such a deplorable condition that the miller's waggons oftentimes stuck in the ruts up to their hubs.

By 1850 Hillfields was a thriving community with 120 ribbon weavers with up to four looms and 13 ribbon manufacturers. Other trades included watchmakers, tile makers, a confectioner, patten and

Looking up Colchester Street in Hillfields in the 1920s, when few owned cars and television hadn't been invented, so no TV aerials. The large building at the end of the street is Singer Cars.

clog makers, a winding engine maker, cobblers, tailors, stone masons and straw bonnet makers in Primrose Hill Street. In the grounds of Primrose Hill House was a high-class boarding school for young gentlemen who could often be seen in their top hats. In 1858–9 Eli Green built his famous triangle of houses here between Berry, Vernon and Brook Street. The 67 houses all had top shops, with looms driven by a single steam engine.

With the increase in population, a church dedicated to St Peter was built of brick on a piece of ground in Canterbury Street given by Charles Weston of Canley, who also laid the foundation stone. It was said that when the church was first built (1841) you could stand at its entrance and look down to Swanswell and the three spires beyond. In the grounds of the church in 1944 a cutting was planted from the famous Glastonbury thorn, said to have grown from the staff of Joseph of Arimathea, in memory of the Revd Paul Stacy who served the parish from 1918.

Through the early 20th century Hillfields had a thriving close-knit community, living mainly in small terraced Victorian houses. However, things changed, for in 1957 Hillfields was designated a Comprehensive Development Area and the landmark tower blocks were built. It was written in *Coventry New Architecture* that, 'No attempt at human scaling appears to have been made, and the bulldozer has been given free rein among the terraces. It is hard to conceive that the same City

Jeffrey Wood's Cross on the curve of Harnall Lane and Swan Lane, photographed in around 1900. (CCL)

Architect's Department has produced the delights and intimacy of Spon End and the sterile megaliths of Hillfields.' Much of the heart of old Hillfields was bulldozed and residents relocated into flats. There are however still some of the original top shops to be seen in Victoria Street.

One building in the area known to generations of Coventrians is the City football ground in Highfield Road. When the club first moved to the site in 1899, it was owned by the Craven Cricket Club, and the football club registered it as Highfield Road despite the fact that it didn't stand in Highfield Road. Highfield Road, which took its name from Highfield Farm, was in fact the nearest place to the original entrance to the site and became the site of the club's main offices. Coventry City began life as the Singer Football Club in around 1883 and quickly became the best team in the city. In 1892 it was proposed that the club represent Coventry and on 12 August 1898 the club secretary received a letter from the Football Association, which read, 'I have now great pleasure in giving consent to your club changing its title from Singer's Football Club to that of Coventry City Football Club.'

One place in Hillfields has an unusual history. Jeffrey Wood's Cross was a place used for the burial of suicides. Those buried here were staked into the ground to stop their spirits rising and if they did rise it was believed that a crossroads held the power to hold the spirit there. Not surprisingly this crossroads had a reputation for being haunted.

Jeffrey Wood's Cross presently stands at the junction of Harnall Lane East, Swan Lane, Burlington Road and Nicholls Street. Originally it was simply the point where Harnall Lane met Swan Lane, originally Tew's Lane, named after the Saxon God of war, Tew. Here we are told that Jeffrey Wood, a suicide, was buried in accordance with the old custom, giving the spot its name. A story from the late 19th century tells of a local family who lived nearby, who were very superstitious. One night, after spending the evening shooting pigeons, a man returned home just after midnight shaking with fear. When he caught his breath he told his family that as he was turning out of the lane towards the Cross, he saw a horse and cart coming towards him driven by a man. The vehicle made no sound whatsoever and as it passed over the crossroads the ground opened and swallowed it. Afterwards members of the family summoned up the courage to visit the Cross at midnight and claimed to have seen the sight over and over again.

Old and new together in a Hillfields street in the early 1960s.

Further Reading
Victoria County History, Vol. 8.
William Gutteridge, *Light and Shadows in an Artisan's Life*.
T.W. Whitley, *Humorous Reminiscences of Coventry Life*.
Grant Lewison and Rosalind Billingham, *Coventry New Architecture*, 1969.
Newspapers, Local Studies.

HOLBROOKS

Holbrooks, meaning the hollow brook, anciently belonged to the parish of Foleshill. The earliest settlement in the parish may have been above Whitmore Park at Park Gate, at the top of Wheelwright Lane, the original settlement of the park keepers. Even in living memory Ivy Cottage, an ancient thatched cottage, stood near the top of the lane, and in the last century other half-timbered thatched cottages stood nearby, scattered around a wooden bridge over the Wyblyno Brook (sometimes called Wyblynd or Wyblyns). Above stood the smithy and below was Holbrook Farm, which had been held by the Holbrook family for centuries. The Wyblyno in fact formed the boundary of the parish, putting the junction of Nunts Lane and Wheelwright Lane in the parish of Exhall. From here the brook heads for Hen Lane, a road which is believed to be of considerable age, the word 'hen' itself meaning 'old.'

Down Hen Lane and into Rowley's Green was a place called 'Wolfpitlydeat' in mediaeval times, probably meaning the wolf pit down the hollow lane. This is one of few references to wolves in the district. In those days the area had a large population of deer, so a pit to catch wolves would have been necessary. Alderman Andrews stated in the late 19th century that the original Hen Lane, which he confirms was a hollow way, lay two miles north of the present road of that name.

Cottages in Parkgate Road were also thatched. The *Coventry Standard* of 1939 tells of Clara Ann Harris, who lived at 113, Parkgate Road:

> *Her cottage had first of all a roof of thatch (spade ace-guineas were found hidden away when the thatch was removed) ... As a girl, to see the farmer's waggon or the doctor's gig go by, was an event in the day's happenings, and it was an even bigger event when 'carriages without horses' passed by. The bridge over the old brook* [Wheelwright Lane], *and later over the level crossing, seemed to mark the very last word in progress.*

Alfred Harris, of the same family as that at Penny Park House, built many properties in the area including the Brookville Cinema (now a pound shop) and apparently it was he who anonymously paid for

Wheelwright Lane in 1935, near its junction with Parkville Highway (Lane) above the bus terminus, still referred to as Ivy Cottage. (CCL)

the great tapestry in the present Coventry Cathedral. Parkgate Road still contains a few Georgian cottages and the Parkgate Hotel, which dates back to 1750. Perhaps the most unusual incident in its history took place in June 1776 when Coventry's thief-taker, Alderman John Hewitt, was searching for William Snow of Little Bowden, who had stabbed his brother-in-law, Thomas Palmer, to death. He wrote:

> *Upon diligent search, agreeable to the instructions I gave to the constables, being continued, Snow was found in bed, at a house a little distant from Coventry, near Penny Park Gate; upon the constables going upstairs, he at first made some resistance, but being shown the coroner's warrant endorsed by me, he submitted.*

Snow was sent to Northampton and there found guilty and hanged.

Wheelwright Lane and Holbrook Lane ran along the eastern boundary of Whitmore Park and up until the Dissolution would have been ditched and fenced. Until World War One Holbrook Lane only supported a dozen cottages, with a clump of them shown in 1887 opposite two large ponds, later the site of the White & Poppe and Dunlop factories. The railway station and crossing were dominant features of the lower end of the parish. The crossing, which was originally gated, was replaced by the present 927ft-long Lockhurst Lane Bridge in 1931. About 300 yards above a cob (mud) cottage stood until World War One, one of the few to survive into the 20th century in Coventry. Another stood in Walsgrave until the 1950s.

The expansion of the rural population was caused mainly by munitions workers living in temporary cottages called Whitmore Park Cottages, Holbrook Lane Cottages (known by the locals as Munition Cottages) and Colony Cottages (all in Whitmore Park). This brought about the

A rare image of a group of ancient mud cottages, which stood in Holbrook Lane before the building of the roadway over the railway. I believe the last cottage of this type in the Coventry area was demolished in Clifford Bridge Road in the early 1950s.

need for a church in the district and a breeze block mission church dedicated to St Luke was built near the corner of Lythall's Lane near the junction with Holbrook Lane in 1916. The recreational needs of the population were served by the opening of Foleshill Park in 1914 (the park actually stands in Whitmore Park), with bowling and putting greens and tennis courts, with bandstands to entertain on summer evenings. Holbrook Lane Cottages were cleared in 1933 for the building of Burnaby Road and Yelverton Road. In Gordon Cowley's *Folkshill* Gladys Young gives her memories of Munition Cottages:

> *We had a good time running through the 'gentrees' as they were called. The shop was situated in the middle. Our cottage faced onto the railway line, which we had to cross to get to the 'Dumps' (the rough ground which contained the semi-underground munition dumps, now Dunlop sports field). We often got a ride on the Tin Lizzie to Courtaulds, whose works used to smell pretty awful.*

After World War One the Ministry of Health gave permission to convert a number of the munition workers' cottages into 738 temporary homes. Gordon Cowley recalled a group of these breeze block cottages below St Paul's Cemetery being demolished in 1938. The last World War One buildings he recalled were hostels between the park and Whitmore Park Cottages, which were kept in use for war workers in World War Two. These, above the park and known as Monks Park Cottages, were still inhabited in the 1950s.

In 1928 the Coventry Stadium, a speedway track, was opened off Lythall's Lane. Those who rode here included the well remembered Stan Petch and British Champion Tommy Fardon, whose unusual speedway-rider memorial stands in St Paul's Cemetery, erected there in 1935 after a fatal crash ended his life prematurely at the age of 24. The track closed in 1936 and the following year a greyhound track opened on the site. This stood until 1964 and was replaced by housing.

In 1939 a new St Luke's Church opened in Rotherham Road, a replica of a church in Paris. The building suffered extensive bomb damage on the night of 14 November 1940, then was restored and reopened in 1944.

Two landmarks of the Rowley's Green end of old Holbrooks were the huge gasholder, which dominated its surrounds until it was demolished in 2002, and the old bone mill. Bedlam Lane, in which the bone mill stood, apparently housed a workhouse in the 18th century, some inmates suffering from mental illness. This gave the lane its name, Bedlam, after the nickname for the famous mental hospital in London.

The rural community of Holbrooks was finally swallowed up by mass house building in the 1930s and 1950s.

Further Reading
Members of St Luke's Church, *Holbrooks History*, 1996.
Gordon Cowley, *Folkshill.*
Various newspapers, Local Studies.

KERESLEY

The name means 'Kaerer's ley', or 'Kaerer's clearing'. It has also been interpreted as 'the Cress Meadow', from the old English '*cerse*'. Keresley was not mentioned in the Domesday Book, but its name appears to be old, including the Danish personal name Kaerer. This is thought to be a relic of the time when the northern half of England was under Danish/Viking control. Other local names associated with Danes are said to be Griff and Biggin. Dugdale states in 1658 in his *History & Antiquities*, 'Returning now to the other side of Coventre, I discern Caresley first in my view; of which I find no mention till K[ing]. Steph.[ens] time … it being then written Keresley.' Interestingly the name is still written exactly the same.

The Tamworth/Keresley Road, which forms the western border of the district, is likely to be an ancient road. It passes the old settlement or camp at Corley Rocks and along its route and in the district Roman coins and objects have been unearthed. The most recent was a coin of Maximian dating to around AD 294, which was dug up in a Keresley garden.

There were two settlements in Keresley, one at Keresley Heath and a second, the older of the two, at Keresley Green. The original settlement was first mentioned in the 12th century when Coventry's lord, Ranulf Gernon, Earl of Chester, granted a chapel here to Coventry Priory. Later that century another Earl of Chester, Ranulf Blundeville, granted woods and waste to the priory. Later a further grant of land was made in 1250 by Roger and Cecily de Montalt.

Other areas not held by the priory belonged to the Wymondswold family, who had land here until 1437. According to Queen's College deeds from at least 1410 the principal building in Keresley was

Looking up the Keresley Road in the 1940s. The photographer is standing close to the site of the long gone Radford Tollgate. The New House stood just off the picture on the right. (CCL)

The New House, Keresley, built by John Hales, as it appeared in 1702, minus its formal Elizabethan gardens.

called Hall Place. Much of the Wymondswolds' estate passed to Queen's College, Oxford, between 1519 and 1529. Other major landowners were the Keresleys, who obviously took their name from the district, who held a large part of the estate in the 13th century. The name continued in the district in later centuries but the families were unrelated.

Some local place-names are extremely old. Pikehorn Wood was known as le Pykehorn in 1338; Bennetts Lane, later road, took its name from John Benyt in 1335. Houndshill, in the northern part of the district, is recorded with that name in 1392 and is associated with a legendary black dog that used to haunt the area. Golden Green was called Goldhordcroft in 1331, probably remembering some ancient treasure being found.

The booklet *Keresley Past and Present*, published in 1944, tells us something of Keresley as it was at the turn of the 20th century. An anonymous contributor known as 'F.H.A.' remembers:

Fifty years ago I came to live in Lower Green [Keresley Green] Keresley. In those days it was a village of few houses, poor roads and no transport. Most children wore heavy nailed boots to keep their feet dry, having so far to go to school. Mr Wright from Manor Farm and my grandfather used to ride ponies to their fields always carrying a tool called a spud. These they used to cut thistles, docks, etc ... I used to go to the Hare and Hounds with a can and sixpence. I used to look at the monkeys there and Mr Clarke would bring the can full of beer, a packet of tobacco and a halfpenny change. Durham House Farm was a farm at that time. Mr John Rotherham [of Keresley Grange] gave the schoolchildren a party every year. This was a great day, tea under a large tree, a hurdy-gurdy playing, races and prize distribution followed.

The Jetty, better known as High Street, Keresley, photographed looking towards the Tamworth Road in around 1910. The cottage on the left still survives but none on the right survived beyond the late 1960s.

The lower village at Keresley Heath once had a Dame School, said to have been in one of the cottages that still exists on the Tamworth Road. In 1852 a Church of England school was built on the corner of the common on land given by Edward Phillips of Whitmore Park. The large and impressive sandstone mediaeval-style school was built with a bell tower near the old gallows site on the corner of Heath.

In 1859 there were 65 boys and 90 girls from Keresley and the surrounding districts of Coundon and Whitmore Park in the school. This declined to 50 in 1875 due to a fall in the local birth-rate and the establishment of other schools. By 1907 the birth-rate had increased again and the number of pupils attending had risen to 150, although the school could only seat around 80!

The school itself was based in a large, upstairs room with an impressive timbered ceiling, which ran the full length of the building. The downstairs served as a house for the schoolmaster and a later wing as the Manager's House. The school served the village for 92 years before being sold in 1962 for £5,600. A block of flats was built on the site.

In September 1847 the Bishop of Worcester consecrated the new church of St Thomas on the Tamworth Road. The church, built in the Decorated style, was erected on land given by local landowner Thomas Troughton. He also supplied the stone, which was quarried from the far corner of the field by the junction of Bennetts Road and Sandpit Lane. The *Coventry Herald and Observer* reported that, 'The weather was fortunately fine and there was present a large attendance, not less than 40 of the Clergymen of the district, besides many of its wealthy and influential inhabitants.'

Keresley and neighbouring Coundon had by the mid-19th century become the most desirable areas for the wealthy to live. Residents included John Rotherham of watch-making fame and William Hillman of Hillman cycles and later motor cars. Hillman lived at Keresley House, which he had converted from a mansion built here in 1816 by William Preest, who sold it soon after its completion. The building later became a convalescent home, then a hospital, and is now the Royal Court Hotel.

One of the most beautiful buildings in the Coventry area once stood at the southern tip of Keresley at the junction of Keresley Road and Sadler Road. This was the New House, which was built on the site of a moated grange built by the Bishop of Coventry in the early 15th century. The original building also served as a hunting lodge as it sat by the entrance to Whitmore Park, the bishop's hunting park.

In 1548 Sir Ralph Sadler acquired the grange and park and sold it on to John Hales, Clerk of the Hanaper, who was speculating on much ex-monastic property in Coventry and came to live at the former friary of Whitefriars. Hales did nothing with the grange but after his death it passed onto his nephew, also known as John Hales. This John wanted to move to the country so he demolished the grange and built a new mansion, calling it the New House. The building was completed in 1586 and faced the Keresley Road. It was surrounded by formal gardens decorated with classical statues. Through over 150 windows were views of the gardens and surrounding countryside including an area on the northern side called 'The Wilderness' and the three spires to the south.

After Hales's death the house passed through various hands including Sir Richard Burnaby, Sir Christopher Yelverton and the Strode family. Until 1720 it was home to the Bohuns, some of whom represented Coventry in Parliament. There is a record of John Bohun's funeral cortège, which left the

Keresley Heath Church of England School in around 1919. The tower on the left originally held a bell and was topped with a small umbrella-like spire. Flats now cover this site on the corner of Tamworth Road and New Street.

New House on 2 December 1699; it consisted of 25 coaches and a hearse, all draped in black. Two hundred large candles burned around his coffin during the service in St Michael's Church.

In 1778 the beautiful house was demolished and on 5 April 1779 the *Coventry Mercury* carried this advert: 'To be Sold at New House, near this City, the remaining part of the Materials of the House, Consisting of a large quantity of Timber, Stone, Tiles, Lead, Glass, Iron &c.'

All that remained of the New House after the demolition were the Keresley Road entrance pillars surmounted by balls. Later a small, 'comfortable' residence was built here which belonged to the

The original Old Shepherd and Shepherdess at Keresley Heath, Keresley. It was this inn that was robbed in the 18th century. The cellar of the building still lies under the car park in front of the present 1936 building.

Hopkins and Smith families until 1816. Afterwards Abraham Barbery Herbert acquired the building and considerably enlarged it, giving it the name 'Moat House.' This building was demolished in the late 1920s and housing sprang up. Nothing now remains of the New House.

The oldest public house in Keresley is the Shepherd and Shepherdess on the Keresley Road. The present building was opened in 1936, built behind the site of the original, which dated to the 18th century. On the evening of 8 April 1790, when the landlord was laid up in bed and his niece was tending him and running the inn, three boisterous men came in.

They called for ale and when she went down into the cellar (which now lies buried behind the No.36 bus stop) she was followed and tied up. The men robbed her of the money she held and her ring, then rifled the downstairs before going upstairs, brandishing pistols, to where the landlord, Mr Humphries, lay. The landlord was put in fear of his life and the men ransacked the upstairs. Their booty consisted of 10 gold guineas, some silver and coppers, clothing, and certain foodstuffs wrapped in linen.

The men then went back down to the cellar where they drank their fill and terrorised their captive. They finally left in high spirits, carrying their plunder over their shoulders down the Keresley Road. The following evening one of the robbers was found asleep in a barn by Radford Bowling Green on Barrs Hill. His accomplices had sneaked off with most of the goods so he was happy to name them. Within four days the other two men were arrested and brought back to Coventry in chains.

After being confined in Coventry Gaol for nearly three months the men were put on trial and capitally convicted for the robbery of the Shepherd and Shepherdess in Keresley. On 18 August 1790, Anthony Farnshaw, aged 56, Thomas Phillips aged 30 and Matthew Archer aged 17 were hanged on Whitley Common before a huge crowd. It is said that Phillips several times urged the executioner to make haste.

When the new inn was built just before the old one closed a reporter from the *Midland Daily Telegraph* visited and spoke to David Osborne, an 82-year-old who had spent his entire life in the village. He recalled the old days: 'Fine place that but it'll never see the sights we saw here. This used to be a big calling place for the farmers. All the horses were tied up outside, and when the farmers had a pint or two we saw some fun.'

He continued:

> No I never had schoolin', I only went but once, and that was in the afternoon to see my pals when the master was out. I went straight to work when I was old enough to stand up. Sometimes I got as much as a shilling a week on the fields ... Like everything else this village has changed ... they used to call this village 'Soap-Suds.' Everybody used to take in washing. It used to be a sight to see the women in poke bonnets and crinolines setting out to fetch the washing from houses for miles around. When they got washing they had to go out to the pit [pond] near the Bell [inn] and get their water in buckets. We all used to work, but the steam laundries beat the washerwomen in the end.

The new Shepherd opened on 31 August 1936 and boasted that it was the only pub in Coventry

Keresley Recreation Ground, Bennett's Road North, in the 1930s. Note the enclosed bandstand and the cricket pitch beyond. Behind can be seen Bunson's Wood and later to the left was built the Keresley Colliery Club.

with revolving doors into the 'vaults.' Mr Osborne was the first to be served in the new inn; shortly afterwards the original inn which stood behind the present bus stop was demolished.

The village's other inns are the Hare and Hounds at Keresley Green, a 19th-century public house standing in its own grounds, and the Bell Inn at Keresley Heath. The Bell was recorded in the census of 1841 as being run by John and Mary Goods, and John was also a sawyer. Living with them was another sawyer, John Thompson, and a five-year-old child, Mary Bentry. From 1880 it was kept by Walter Probert, a farmer. Being both a farmer and an ale-house keeper was quite common. By 1908 Walter was recorded as, 'Bell Inn, and farmer, and collector of poor rates and King's taxes.' Walter died in 1912 and his stone can be seen in St Thomas's churchyard.

The population of Keresley Green and Heath was mainly employed in agriculture, until in 1917 the Warwickshire Coal Company hit a coal seam some 23ft 10in thick at 720 yards depth. This was the start of over 60 years of mining above Keresley Green and the development of the modern Keresley village. The Coventry Colliery, as it came to be known, raised one million tons of coal between 1923 and 1929. In 1927 it was recorded that huge quantities of water were being pumped from the colliery and all the wells within 3,000 yards had dried up. Production of coal continued to increase and later the Homefire plant, which made smokeless fuel, was built nearby. Both are now gone and have been replaced by the Prologis Business Park.

One area of interest in Keresley is Penny Park. This and nearby Park Gate appear to have originated as dwellings housing the prior's men, who kept the hunting park in order. One old house in Penny Park, which still survives, stands on the corner of Penny Park and Nunts Lane. The unusual

Keresley Colliery and Homefire plant structures, which dominated Keresley Village for much of the 20th century.

stone building, known as Penny Park House, has now been converted into two dwellings, but was once a large farmhouse. It is connected to Edward Broome, whom legend tells was hanged in the Old Barn, which once stood nearby. It is said that sometime in the 16th century the owner of Penny Park House was John Shore. Shore invited a number of worthies to a feast at his home. They included Elizabeth Sadler of Newland Hall, to whom he was about to become engaged. He also invited his near neighbour Edward Broome, who also had designs on Elizabeth. As she rode to the house with her servants she was accosted by Broome, who begged her to elope with him on horseback. She refused, Broome grabbed her horse's bridle, it reared and Elizabeth fell to the floor. She lay there as if dead and Broome panicked and fled, accompanied by his faithful dog. Elizabeth was carried back to Penny Park House and Shore, believing she was dead, rode in pursuit of Broome with a number of men. They found him, for he wasn't trying to escape, although his dog fought to protect his master and was killed. Broome said nothing as he was taken to the barn, where he was hanged from a chain. Shore and his men were glad but horrified to see that Elizabeth was alive and well when they returned. It is said that the truth was covered up and it was believed that Broome had accidentally killed himself while drunk. How the truth eventually got out is unknown.

After the event Broome's ghost and the ghost of his dog were often seen in the area and became well known in the Keresley and Whitmore Park area. The story of Broome's ghost was resurrected in the early 20th century by Alfred Harris, who restored Penny Park House. It is said he did it to create more interest in the Old Barn, which had become a centre of community life and had raised much for good causes, including £2,500 for Keresley Hospital. Its greatest moment was in 1938 when the Duke of Kent paid a visit.

The ghost of Broome's dog does however appear to be linked to an older story concerning a huge supernatural black dog that walked through the 'Dog Land' and Shuckmore (the Demon's Moor) in Radford, through Whitmore Park to Hounds Hill at the northern tip of Keresley. It was due to this creature that no one would pass through Whitmore Park at night.

It is said to have been seen in the late 18th century by a horseman, on his way home from the local inn. He struck out at the beast with his riding crop and it exploded in a flash of light, leaving the man lying in a ditch with the clothes burned off his back. His horse was found in a terrible state two days later. The dog was later seen in Bennett's Road North, by the Long Meadow (near Durham House Farm), in the middle of the 19th century. A local farm worker was bringing two shire horses from the meadow one morning when they froze in their tracks. A huge black dog, about the size of a pony, walked by. As the creature passed it looked around and appeared to grin, baring its huge teeth. It disappeared in a hedge in a burst of light, startling the horses. Similar events have reportedly occurred in practically every county in England.

The creature was last seen in 1949 by Mr. J., who worked at the water pumping station in Watery Lane. At 2am one morning he was crossing the Top Meadow to check the pump when his way was blocked by a huge black dog. The creature sat staring as he shone his lamp into its eyes and as he edged around it he noted that it followed him, turning its head and staring. The creature was huge; it sat down and measured over 5ft 10in. Once he had passed it he ran back to the pump room and locked himself in. Next day he told his mate who came to relieve him, and shortly afterwards a neighbour called them over to see a pad print in his garden 'about the size of a dinner plate'. Mr. J. was in his 80s when he told this story; he hadn't bothered to tell anyone but his wife, because he said 'No-one would believe me.'

Further Reading
Keresley & Coundon Women's Institute, *Just Amongst Ourselves*, 1988.
The Keresley & District War Memorial Appeals Committee, *Keresley: Past, Present and Future*, c.1947.
Coventry Mercury 1790.
Various newspaper cuttings, Local Studies.

LONGFORD

The name Longford, meaning 'the long ford', has been found by Roman place-name researchers to be common along Roman roads. The Longford/Foleshill Road may be a remnant of a Roman road that passed through Coventry. The route can be traced from Mancetter/Bedworth through Coventry, linking up around the Lunt Fort area. A few years ago a coin of Claudius, who invaded Britain in AD 43, was unearthed near the road in Longford Park. Even in 1942 it was said that a Roman road passed through another part of Longford, 'by the old kilns close to Tackley Waste and through the Moat House, Exhall.' The present roads once had toll houses and gates – one was said to be at the corner of Vine Cottage and the second stood opposite Windmill Road amid open fields and copses.

Until the early part of the 20th century, before it became a separate ward, Longford was described as a hamlet in the civic parish of Foleshill. Part of it was also known as Tackley, but over a period of time that name disappeared. Another part of Longford is also known as Foxford, which takes its name from the fact that across the meadows from the Long Ford was another ford called Short Ford. It was said that in the fields near Short Ford the largest fox ever seen was once chased. The animal ran through the ford and thereafter it bore the name. Also to commemorate the event an inn was opened called The Fox. This was demolished when Foxford Council School, built in 1875, was extended.

A report in the *Coventry Standard* from 1942 described the hamlet thus:

> *It has altered considerably during the past thirty years or so, for in the centre of the district, in addition to the Parish Church of St Thomas, built in 1874, with schools nearby and the Coach and Horses and the Saracen's*

Alderman's Green Road in the 1930s. (CCL)

Woodshires Green Road, photographed in 1925. The place began life as one of the district's many small hamlets and was swallowed by development between the wars. (CCL)

Head Inns exactly opposite, there have been built a block of shops, a skating rink and a billiards hall, and a short distance away, a new housing estate has been opened out; all of which together with rows of new and old houses and shops, a modernised Griffin Inn, and the Post Office and branches of Lloyds, Barclays and Midland Banks, present a pleasing picture to the eye.

Across the road from St Thomas's Church is Market Square, at one time the shopping centre, where tradesmen did a brisk trade. But many of the older inhabitants of Longford associate the spot with Longford Wake, when booths and stalls and various amusements, such as roundabouts, shooting galleries and swing boats lined the open street in Market Square, and in front of the Coach and Horses and even down the main road as far as Mr. Masser's House, now Longford Post Office.

Longford Wake used to take place in the third week in August. As a special treat the locals ate Christmas fare: roast beef and plum pudding. In front of the Saracen's Head could always be found the 'cheap-jack', selling china, cutlery, cheap jewellery from Birmingham and other fancy goods. The cheap-jack also organised competitions in which the contestants had their hands tied behind their backs and had to eat huge dumplings covered in treacle. By the end of the 19th century the wake was so big that it caused problems for anyone trying to pass by on the road. In around 1900 it was moved to Wright's Field on the main Longford Road, by the Long Ford.

One of the area's earliest recorded industries was coal mining, which began in 1682 at Hawkesbury. During the 19th century many Long and Foxfordians were weavers. Some were outworkers for Thomas Stevens of Stevengraph fame in Coventry. In 1942 it was reported that a certain Mrs Moore lived opposite the staff entrance to the school in a house built by her forebears that contained a large silk weaving shop. About 50 yards further on, on the corner of Jackers Road, was another large weaving shop. There it was reported that:

> *The father and grandfather of septuagenarian Mr Albert Johnson made beautiful silk bookmarkers for Mr Stevens, of Cox Street, Coventry. Some of the bookmarkers had the Lord's Prayer and the Belief woven into them, and Mr. Johnson's firm was one of the two weaving places capable of turning out these delicate designs.*

One of the most flourishing companies in Longford arrived in 1920 when the Longford and Midland Concrete Company on the Bedworth Road was set up by George Millerchip. The company specialised in making concrete blocks for canal locks, paving slabs and kerbs, and at their Grindle Road yard they made ornamental stonework for the building trade. It is said that before World War Two most of Coventry was paved by the company. During the war the company supplied all-concrete air-raid shelters to Coventry, Birmingham, Stratford, Nuneaton, Rugby, Oxford and Banbury.

Another well-known Longford firm was the Foleshill Brick and Tile Works, founded by Albert Johnson in Sydnall Road in 1897, near the Longford and Exhall railway station. Another noted industry was boat-building on the canal, mainly carried out by members of the noted Sephton family in their yard by the old engine house at Hawkesbury Junction, better known as Sutton Stop, and at Tusses Bridge. It is said a Sephton boat could carry one ton more than any other boat of equivalent size.

Sutton Stop has always been an important stopping point for canal users past and present, for here the Coventry and Oxford canals once ran side by side. Longford Wharf (now gone), where the Oxford Canal formerly joined the Coventry Canal on the Longford Road, was the first wharf established by the Coventry Canal Company and the first coal to arrive here from the Bedworth coalfield came in 1768. From this wharf coal was taken by waggon to Coventry and the surrounding districts, as the canal did not reach the city itself until 1769. Cottages and shops developed in Hollybush Lane to serve the wharf and junction. Also at the wharf was a shallow lock – the Oxford Canal was always six inches higher than the Coventry Canal. From here to Sutton Stop the two canals ran side by side, because the canal companies could not agree the tolls. It was not until 1802 that the problem was resolved and the junction was made at Sutton Stop. The old Oxford Canal was not filled in until the late 20th century.

The canal passes under Grange Road Bridge with its high humped back, one of two once found here. The bridge was formerly known as Coney Lane Bridge. This may imply that there was once a large rabbit population here, or it may be a reference to the humped back of the bridge, which is like the back of a seated rabbit.

The present Grange Road, named after nearby Grange Farm, was the birthplace of noted trade union leader Tom Mann. He was born in 1856 at 177 Grange Road, an early 19th-century cottage, now a Grade II listed building. His father was a clerk at the Victoria Colliery and his mother died

The iron bridge over the canal at Sutton Stop, also known as Hawkesbury Junction, photographed in around 1910. (CCL)

when he was very young. Tom spent only three years at school, leaving when he was nine to work for a year, possibly as a bird-scarer at Grange Farm. At the tender age of 10 young Tom went down the pit, dragging tubs of coal down narrow passages by a chain fixed to his waist. When he was 14 there was a fire at the pit and Tom and his father left and moved to Birmingham, where he became an apprentice toolmaker. After his apprenticeship Tom moved to London where he joined the craft guild of the Amalgamated Society of Engineers.

In those days unions had very limited membership and Tom worked to improve the situation. He became one of the leaders of the Great Dock Strike of 1889 and helped to form the Dockers' Union. He also worked for the reduction of working hours and for the rights of the low paid. He became the General Secretary of the Independent Labour Party, working with Ramsey MacDonald and Kier Hardy to help create the Labour Party. Tom became a founder member of the Communist Party in 1920 and met Lenin in Moscow the following year. Many of his comrades became MPs but Tom could not settle for making speeches and 'agitated' across five continents, being imprisoned several times, the last time when he was 75. Tom Mann was still stirring things up for the good of the working man in Sweden at the age of 83. The boy from Longford certainly made his mark on the world.

Sutton Stop is named after Richard Sutton, a toll clerk and wharfinger for the Oxford Canal Company between 1769 and 1846. His son Henry also held the position until the 1870s and both are buried at the United Reform Church yard in Old Church Road, Foleshill.

Many of the cottages at Sutton Stop were originally built for colliers rather than canal workers. The Greyhound pub is first mentioned in the 1820s, when the owner was Thomas Worthy, described as a farmer. Later he is described as a farmer and innkeeper. It was not uncommon for farmers to run pubs as a sideline; some even took payment for fishing rights and threw in bread and cheese!

A landmark at the Stop is the beautiful iron bridge, which was designed by John Sinclair of the Coventry Canal Company. It was cast at the Britannia Foundry in Derby and erected in 1837 at a cost of £525. The bill was paid by the Coventry Canal Company as the Oxford Canal Company could not agree to a payment.

The Stop's other famous landmark is the engine house built by the Coventry Canal Company at the beginning of the 19th century. In 1821 a second-hand steam-powered Newcomen engine was purchased and installed and called *Lady Godiva*. The purpose of the engine was to top up the canal. In 1837 a second 25hp engine was installed alongside and called the *Earl of Mercia*. To accommodate both the engine house was enlarged and a new larger chimney added. In 1904 the original well was deepened to almost 100ft, believed to be the deepest in Warwickshire. In 1913 the water failed, although it was not a problem as water was available from the mains and the pumps became redundant.

During World War Two *Earl of Mercia* was sold and *Lady Godiva* was later removed by the Newcomen Society. It was restored, and in 1963, to commemorate Newcomen's 300th anniversary, it was put on display at the Thomas Newcomen Museum in Dartmouth. The engine house still stands although it is in a poor condition.

In the past local religion was associated with the canal. On Lady Lane (formerly Canal Road) stands Longford Salem Baptist Chapel, originally built in 1765 and rebuilt in 1807. Adults who were to be baptised were taken from the chapel draped in white cloth and baptised in the nearby canal. In the cold winter of 1865 it is said that the canal ice had to be broken to accommodate four baptisms. Soon after the chapel had a baptistery created indoors.

Few incidents in Longford's history are recorded, mainly because the area consisted of farms and scattered houses. One of the few remembered is the robbery committed in September 1821 by a miner named Moore and a weaver called Butcher. These two young men broke into Stonebrook Farm, the residence of Mr Owen, a local farmer, stole £20 and in the process seriously injured their victim. Despite making their escape the law caught up with them after they had been tracked through the area at Idle Lane, Waggoner's Overthrow and Hawkesbury Stop. The men were captured, put on trial and sentenced to death. Shortly before their execution their victim, Mr Owen, visited them in Coventry Gaol. The men sought his forgiveness and Mr Owen offered what consolation he could. Both men belonged to a religious group known as the 'Ranters' and at seven o'clock on the morning of their execution they had a statement read out which said:

> We hope that none will upbraid the denomination called the 'Ranters' on account of our conduct, for it was not them that occasioned us to come here, for had we done as they taught us we might have been happy men with our families. This we intended to have declared at the place of execution, but less we should not be able, we declare it this morning, before we go to the fatal spot.

The handsome Mission church of St Matthew in Lenton's Lane was built in 1895 mainly from corrugated iron. Concrete was later added. I believe the building was based on a Saxon church in Greensted, Essex. Sadly this rather unusual building was closed in 1963 and demolished and the site is now covered by housing. (CCL)

Later that morning they were taken to Whitley Common seated on their coffins and hanged before a crowd of thousands. Friends removed their bodies and took them for burial at Bedworth. Stonebrook Farm lay unoccupied for many years and gained a reputation as a haunted house. When a tenant was eventually found he had to be given the first year rent-free. Thereafter the farm prospered under various tenants, including the Elds, Wrights and Ashmores.

A noted prizefight took place in Longford in November 1830, in a field near the Engine public house. The combatants were John (Jack) 'Fatty' Adrian and Bill Betteridge, for 40 sovereigns. The *Herald* reported that Betteridge was a much bigger man, some seven inches taller than Adrian. Despite this 'Jack gave the first knock-down blow, showing himself the best fighter, placing at least half a dozen blows to his opponent's one.' Betteridge however drew first blood and on many occasions had Jack held around the head while he worked on his body. The fight lasted for 103 rounds, lasting 2½ hours before the 'beaks' stopped it. It was afterwards claimed that this was a ruse as Adrian was the favourite and Betteridge was gaining the upper hand. There may have been some substance in the claim for afterwards Betteridge claimed the purse and received it.

Further Reading
Coventry Canal Society, *Coventry's Waterway: A City Amenity*, 1972.
Various newspaper cuttings, Local Studies.
Coventry Herald, 12 November 1830.

RADFORD

The name comes from the Anglo-Saxon 'Raed-ford,' meaning the red ford. Disturbed clay in the stream bed would have turned the ford water a ruddy red colour. Radford's history is closely tied to Coventry, as its southern tip runs into the city centre. Little is known for certain of its pre-Conquest history. A coin known as a Gallo-Beligic gold stater, dating from 57–45 BC was found in a garden in Beake Avenue and is now on display at the museum. Barrs Hill, thought by some to have taken its name from the mediaeval Bishop's Bar or Gate, is believed by others to have taken its name from the Celtic 'barr' meaning hilltop. There is evidence that the hilltop may have been a hill fort. A deed granted to Isabell Kyrvyne in 1577 refers to this area. The churchwardens of Holy Trinity granted her 'two barns and two closes lying in Medelborowe ways leading from Coventre towards Radeforde'. The word Medelborowe comes from the ancient British word for fortification, and survives as Middleborough Road.

A mid-18th century prospect of Coventry shows the hillside with escarpments cut into it and until the mid-19th century a covered sunken track survived on the west side of the hill. This was of a type normally found on hill forts and led down the hillside to the Radford Brook. It was wide enough for one man to walk down without being seen. The Holloway was filled in the late 19th century. This track may have been part of the lane recorded in the 16th century as Lideat Lane, which crossed the hill from east to west. The name itself suggests a connection, for in Middle English it means 'the covered path'.

There appears to have been activity on Barrs Hill in the Roman period. A local legend states that a Roman general called Agricola built a camp on the hill and named the local settlement (Coventry) after the water goddess Coventina. Agricola was indeed a Roman general and governor of Britain. The hilltop has yielded Roman pottery and coins from the 1st to 4th century, as at the Lunt at Baginton. Roman objects have also been found at the hill's base in Coventry, including a statuette, hippo-sandals (horseshoes) and a quern. These were found near a 200ft causeway built to carry men and horses across the ancient seasonal lake which once separated Barrs Hill from Broadgate Hill, the centre of Coventry.

Looking up the Radford Road in the late 19th century. On the left now lies the parade of shops, converted from normal housing. Part of the wall on the right, which belonged to a Victorian villa, still stands outside the Radford Social Club. (CCL)

The original Grapes Inn on the Radford Road (Barrs Hill) in the early 1930s. This building was later replaced by the present building opposite in Bridgeman Road.

In 1279 two estates in Radford were held by Roger de Montalt, Thomas de Adern and Coventry Priory. By 1411 the priory had gained more land in the district and had some 20 tenants. After the Dissolution the priory's land in Radford was acquired by Richard Andrews, Leonard Chamberlain and the Coventry Corporation. The north of Radford was bounded by a ditched fence, the boundary of the prior's old hunting park, Whitmore Park, and the east side was bounded by the Endemere (Springfield brook) as far as the ancient Cunnetford. Some of Radford's ancient field names are now street names, including Cramper's Field, Priors Field and Ashmore. Forgotten names include Upper and Lower Shuckmore, the high and low ground of the village, around Lydgate Hill. The name derives from the Anglo-Saxon '*scucca*' meaning demon and appears to be connected to another area on the southern edge of Radford called the 'Dog Land.' This appears to be connected to a legendary black dog, which roamed here and in Whitmore Park and Keresley.

Radford has had three churches in its history dedicated to St Nicholas. The first stood on the site of the later Trinity Vicarage which stood at the top of St Nicholas Street. The origins of the church are unknown (there is a tradition that St Chad set up a chapel here) but dates back to at least the late Saxon period. It is believed that the first church, which was supported in the mediaeval period by the Corpus Christi and St Nicholas guilds, had two towers or steeples, for fields nearby were known as the 'Little' and 'Big' steeple fields. The church's importance is reflected by the fact that it housed up to 15 chaplains to perform the various ceremonies. The local historian Mary Dormer Harris wrote in 1913:

A typical Sunday afternoon in Naul's Mill Park in Edwardian times. (CCL)

> *I remember Canon Beaumont saying that it was no unusual thing for the gardener to find bones there when he was digging; indeed he once found a human body in an extraordinary state of preservation, only it almost immediately crumbled to dust.*

The church, which stood on Barrs Hill overlooking the city, was destroyed in the 16th century after the dissolution of the guilds in 1547. Dugdale states that in the 17th century nothing remained of the building, although it was noted in 1933 that steps and a plinth remained in the vicarage garden. Many of the old cottages in the village had sandstone bases and when two very old houses were demolished on the corner of Lydgate Road remains of ancient worked stones and a column were found.

The second church was built in Radford village and consecrated in 1874. The church was built of local stone quarried from the grounds of Westfield House and built in the early English style as a chapel to Holy Trinity Church. In its churchyard were buried many notables including A.E. Stoddart, friend of W.G. Grace and captain of the Ashes-winning England cricket team of the 1890s. Henry Sturmey, motor man, editor of *The Autocar* and inventor of the Sturmey-Archer

A mid-19th century painting of Cash's famous model factory, built at Kingfield next to the Coventry Canal. (CCL)

The Victorian church of St Nicholas in Radford, photographed in around 1900. Nothing of this building now survives. (CCL.)

gears, also lies here, along with John George Wood, England's most popular Victorian natural historian and author of over 70 books on natural history.

On the night of 14 November 1940 my father witnessed a land mine explode above the church. Nothing survived of the building and many of the graves that surrounded it. A number of firewatchers were trapped under the rubble of the completely flattened building; four died along with the curate. My father Cyril, once he recovered from the blast, helped to rescue the survivors.

The present church was built near to the site of the old one in 1955 in modern style and was the first new church to be consecrated after the war. It contains the font of the previous church and houses the bells in an unusual tall brick campanile. Before it stands the small village war memorial presented to the village by Vernon Pugh of Radford House. This originated across the road on the common and was moved to its present position in the 1980s.

The once well-known Radford Spring in the centre of the village was noted throughout the Coventry area as a source of healing water. It stood in a field on land later belonging to Spring Farm. The original Radford Spring, called the 'Saxon Well' by many locals, was within a circle of stones and from the 17th century was tightly capped by a large glacial boulder, known as the Radford Boulder. The boulder was carved with the initials A.K., because in around 1675 the Kings, a family of brewers, had a lead pipe laid from the well to their brewery in King Street. When access to this water was stopped people used the spring water, which bubbled up through a sand bed in the Radford Brook a few yards away. This may have been a separate spring or the capping of the spring in the 17th century may have forced some of the water to divert into the nearby brook.

In the 19th century the farmer began to tire of hordes of people on his land using the spring and had it piped to a trough by the road, just below the churchyard. It was later piped to an outlet set into the wall on the spring side of the road by Spring House. Whether this water came from the brook or well is not known, but the boulder was removed for a short time in the late 19th century, no doubt for this work to take place. Inside the well a 17th-century lead suction rose was found from the brewery pipe. The outlet on the Radford Road was constantly in use and one lady interviewed in 1936 said:

I have seen as many as five people at the spring bathing their ankles in the water when they had sprained them badly. People used to come from all parts of the town to bathe their joints or to carry water back home to bathe their eyes. I remember that it was the regular custom for new-born babies to have their first wash from water drawn from this spring.

This description is interesting for the cures, especially for joints and eyes, are associated with pre-Christian sacred wells. The washing of new-borns in spring water was also practiced by the pagan Saxons. The well no doubt had a very ancient history, and may have originated as a pagan spring dedicated to a forgotten god or goddess, maybe Coventina herself. Whenever it snowed the snow above the pipe that carried the water always

A rare mid-19th-century engraving of the Radford Tollgate, which once stood on the Radford Road near the site of the present roundabout at the start of Keresley Road.

melted and in the 1930s it was noted that the water maintained a higher temperature than the atmosphere. Despite this those who remember the spring say that in the summer the water was always ice cold. When the area was built up in 1936 the spring was built over and the water diverted into the main sewer. Another spring could until recently be seen trickling across the pavement on the corner of Radford Common.

Summer Row on the Radford Road opposite Radford Common during a flood in the 1940s. The building protruding at the end of the row is the beginning of another block of cottages called Bambury's Buildings.

A drawing by Florence Weston showing Naul's Mill in Radford as it was in the 19th century.

Development of the land meant that the Saxon well was covered in 1913, but it continued to feed the water supply in the wall. The syenite granite Radford Boulder, fixed to the sandstone well by iron staples, was a Coventry landmark which many believed marked the centre of England. It weighed about half a ton, and was thought to have been carried from Leicestershire thousands of years before by glacial movement. In October 1913 it was removed and blown up with dynamite, much to the horror of locals and historians who saved what they could and had it reassembled and placed in the churchyard. In 1940 it was destroyed by the landmine blast.

Spring House was a farmhouse and was the only farm in the village. It was farmed in the late 19th century by Joseph Warden and his son Joseph. It was a large farm, extending east of the Radford Road across almost to Holbrook Lane. The late Bill Glover recalls: 'Mr Warden and his family were regular worshippers at St Nicholas. Every year on 'Care Away' (curds and whey) Sunday at Lent it was customary to buy curds and whey from the farm.'

Below Spring House was Radford House, set within beautiful gardens and boasting its own summerhouse. Radford House originated as a much smaller building and was the home of David Spencer, a silk weaving manufacturer, in 1830. In the early part of the reign of Queen Victoria it was converted into a Catholic school with its own chapel. It most noted pupil was Sir Henry Tichborne, who married Mary Petre of Whitley Abbey at St Osburg's Church. Sir Henry nearly lost his title, because his predecessor Sir Roger Tichborne disappeared at sea in 1854 and another claimed his title and caused a national sensation. A large man (Roger was thin) returned to England claiming to be Sir Roger and was believed by the aged Lady Tichborne, but not by the rest of the

Barr's Hill Girls' School, the former home of John Kemp Starley, before World War One. (CCL)

family. He claimed the Tichborne estate and toured England pressing his cause. This included a trip to Coventry where he appeared at the Britannia Music Hall. His claim went to the courts and 'Sir Roger' was proved to be Arthur Orton from Wapping and he was given a prison sentence. Despite this some continued to support him and he was later buried under the name of Sir Roger Tichborne.

Radford House in 1912, originally the home of silk man Mark Spencer in the 1830s and later the Radford Hotel public house. (CCL)

The house became the home of the De Creeses, who sold it to county family the Pughs in 1900. The head of the household was Vernon Pugh, managing director of the Rudge-Whitworth cycle company. Vernon's son Lieutenant 'Dickie' Pugh was a naval man and shipmate of Prince George, the Duke of Kent, who made many personal visits to Radford House in the 1920s.

In 1929 Radford House was sold first to Atkinson's Brewery and then to Mitchell's and Butler's. It became the Radford Hotel. In those early days locals played cricket behind the pub and sat in its huge garden as the old summerhouse gradually fell into decay. The last early 19th-century large building from the old village of Radford was shamefully vandalised before being demolished in 2002.

Another building of interest was Barrs Hill House, home of John Kemp Starley, nephew of the 'Father of the Cycle,' James Starley. History tells us that J.K. was the inventor of the first real safety cycle, known as the 'Rover' and on which all modern cycles are based. In 1908 the house and its beautiful grounds became Barrs Hill Girls' School, the first fee-paying secondary school in the city. It remained a girls' school into the 1970s when it was turned into a mixed comprehensive. The old house was then demolished and turned into a car park, despite promises to the contrary.

Below Barrs Hill House in a valley lies the present Naul's Mill Park, with its large boating pond. The original mill on the Radford Brook (where it crosses Abbott's Lane) was in existence by the 12th century. It bore many names such as Wragg's or Carter's Mill and was used as a fulling mill and flour mill. After the Corporation bought the mill in 1889 the mill pond was drained and the mill demolished. Within a few years the entire mill pond site had been buried and on its site Corporation stables were built. In 1899 it was proposed to turn Naul's Mill Meadow (not on the original site of the mill) into a public park, but it was not until 12 April 1909 that the park, with its newly constructed pool, opened.

In 1848 horse racing came to an end in Stoke and moved permanently to Radford. There had been steeplechase races here, starting from below Barrs Hill and held over open land, from as early as 1843. An 80ft stand was erected on the hillside from which observers could see the entire race. Steeplechases over fence, ditch and hedge resumed permanently in 1849 in the Conduit Meadows and consisted of eight races held over two days. The races drew 8–10,000 spectators and many used the railway embankment as a vantage point, as the races took place below them and finished alongside Barker Butts Lane. The *Coventry Standard* of 1849 reported that it was 'considered by competent judges as being one of the best courses in the kingdom.'

In 1852 a new flat course was completed measuring just over one mile and it too was one of the best in the country. In 1860 jockey John Ennis, riding a horse called Poet, fell at the last hurdle and was struck in the chest by another horse. He died three days later. Soon after this racing stopped at Radford and was not resumed until 1874. In the first race the famed jockey Fred Archer rode and won the Packington Nursery Plate on Anina and on the following day won on Agar. The new races, however, suffered because Coventry's puritans objected to betting and the pickpockets and fraudsters attracted to the course. Despite new rules from the Jockey Club the races finally ended in 1876. Much of the racecourse was afterwards divided into allotments, with the idea that Radford would become Coventry's main market garden.

Radford was also the site of another more violent sporting occasion, which likewise drew thousands, the prizefight. Coventry's most noted fighter Paddy Gill, who one could say was an early national champion, had his first fight on Radford Common against Bill Heaps for £5.

Although Radford has always been a rural farming district, in 1838 two-thirds of the population were involved in weaving. Top shops existed until the late 1960s on the main Radford Road as part of a group of old houses on a raised bank, which included the old Buck and Crown public house. In 1857 Quakers John and Joseph Cash built their handsome houses-cum-workshops by the canal in the far east of the district at Kingfield. Cash's specialise in silk weaving on Jacquard looms and later claimed justifiably to have 'labelled the world' by producing name labels. They are also notable for their silk pictures, which were based on an idea originated in the 19th century by Coventry's Thomas Stevens. The late Lois Charles was born at No.1 Kingfield in 1904. She recalls:

I remember as a schoolgirl being quite embarrassed by living in a house surmounted by a workshop in which looms clattered noisily from 6.30am to 6.30pm ... Due to the shortage of work caused by the influx of French textiles there was not enough to employ all the cottage weavers ... so the workshops over the cottages were opened up into one continuous workshop called the 'Longshop.' In front of each house was a garden ... Each one was composed of flower beds ... surrounded by low box hedges ... Each year the Cash family gave a prize for the best garden.

Radford is also the birthplace of the nation's motor car industry. In 1896 Harry Lawson acquired an old burnt-out cotton mill in Draper's Field and converted it into what he called 'Motor Mills.' It

A rare photograph showing the first Daimler BE12 about to take off from Radford Aerodrome in 1915. (CCL)

was here that the Great Horseless Carriage Company and the Daimler Company produced the first English-built cars in July–August 1897. Later the works would be solely used by Daimler, who extended onto the Stripes Farm site further up Sandy Lane in 1922. The original works were not entirely vacated until 1937. The Daimler Road Factory off Sandy Lane was vacated in the late 1990s and is now a new housing estate called Daimler Green.

During World War One Daimler also built aircraft, including the BE 12 fighter. These flew directly from the factory, from what became Radford Aerodrome. In a letter written by the mother of Bob Ashmore, dated 30 March 1914, she writes: 'Yesterday another aeroplane came down bang and the lieutenant killed. That makes six poor fellows who have been burnt to death around here in the last three weeks.' Planes flew from here in 1917 in an attempted to intercept a German zeppelin, which dropped bombs in the grounds of Whitley Abbey and Baginton Sewage Farm. The aerodrome also housed a prisoner of war camp.

The Radford Aerodrome Estate was built over much of the area in the 1930s and during World War Two some of the airfield still existed, providing a take-off point for more Daimler-built aircraft and providing a temporary home for a small group of Spitfires. The aerodrome once had another notable feature, a massive concrete butt, created in the 19th century and used by the army and volunteers as an 800-yard rifle range. The butt, although overgrown with moss, was also used in World War One. However, when one target-marker was accidentally killed by a deflected bullet in September 1915, it was demolished.

The farmland which surrounded Radford village was first built upon by the Radford Housing Estate off Moseley Avenue. The land was purchased by the Corporation in 1924 for £45,000, some of which was sold to private builders for £86,000. Just after this the Hill Farm Estate was built on land belonging to Hill Farm in the north-east. The Radford Aerodrome Estate followed, in which many old names were used including Stripes Road, and Stripes Fields, derived from Stripes Farm, and Warden Road was named after the Wardens of Spring Farm. Grangemouth Road takes its name from one of the entrances to Grange Farm, which disappeared just after the war. Telfer Road takes its name from William Telfer of the Warwickshire Coal Company, who once owned the land, and the local shopping centre, Jubilee Crescent, was designed in the Jubilee year of King George V. One reminder of World War One is Guardhouse Road, for when the White & Poppe munition factory was guarded in the war, the guardhouse was sited near to the top of this road.

Finally we cannot leave Radford before mentioning Charles Bray. Bray was a ribbon manufacturer and newspaper owner who lived with his wife Caroline, also known as Cara, at Rosehill, a Victorian villa on the site of the present Coachmaker's Club on the Radford Road. In November 1841 Mary Ann Evans, later to become the famed novelist George Eliot, was brought to Rosehill by her next-door neighbours the Pears.

This was the turning point in the young woman's life; she soon began to question her religious beliefs and to meet notables who visited Rosehill, including the novelist William Makepeace Thackeray, who wrote part of his novel *The Newcomes* there. Rosehill was a centre of the intelligentsia

Not a Daimler, as often thought, but a Great Horseless Carriage Company vehicle photographed with Francis Baron, the works manager, at the wheel in 1897. (CCL)

in Coventry, where ideas concerning religion, philosophy, socialism and so on were freely discussed.

Charles Bray encouraged Mary Ann into the world of literature and published her work in his newspaper, the *Coventry Herald*. George Eliot the writer was literally born in Coventry. After her father's death she stayed permanently at Rosehill before leaving for London. From there she

'Rosehill', home of Charles and Cara Bray.

later wrote to Cara's sister Sarah Hennell 'Sometimes it seems a little while since you and I were walking over Radford Fields, with the youth in our limbs, talking and laughing with the easy companionship, which it is difficult to find in later life.'

In those early days Mary Ann was somewhat taken with Bray, who was known as the 'Don Juan of Coventry'. She referred to him as the, 'dear unmanageable male unit in our quarternian,' indicating that he was the centre of attention of Mary Ann, Cara and Sarah Hennell. Bray retired in 1856, which resulted in a halving of his yearly income to £400 a year. He was forced to sell Rosehill to John Cash and in 1857 the Brays moved into Ivy Cottage, a smaller residence within the grounds, which they shared with Sarah Hennell. Despite Bray's decline in fortune the churchwarden's accounts for 1860 show that Trinity Church sold him land on Barrs Hill, for which he paid £4,000 in cash on 16 March. In 1861 the Brays moved to Barrs Hill Terrace, a group of four-storey terraced properties which still stand. By 1891 Charles had died and Cara and Sarah were back at Ivy Cottage, which had been leased to the minister of West Orchard Chapel. It is said that George Eliot offered help to her friends when money was short, although her offer was refused. She did convince Cara to accept £50 as an advance for a children's story.

Charles Bray had a second family he kept in Radford village that went under the name of Gray. Mrs Hannah Gray claimed to be married to a travelling man. She once worked as cook at Rosehill and her daughter Nellie, one of six children she had with Bray, lived at Rosehill as the daughter of Charles and Cara. Nellie died when she was 20.

Further Reading

The Victoria History of the County of Warwick, Volume VIII 74–76, 366.

Lois Charles, *Memories of my Childhood Years at Cash's*.

Miscellaneous newspaper cuttings, Local Studies Centre.

Census, 1881 and 1891.

SPON END

The name means 'the end of a district', from the Old English '*spanna*', a length or measurement of land. Spon End begins at Spon Bridge, or Spon End Bridge, at the end of Spon Street, and ends around Four Pounds Avenue. The area is an extension of the 12th-century suburb of Coventry once called Spanna or Spon. The lower part of Spon End towards the Butts once contained many ancient timbered buildings, mostly demolished in the late 1930s. The Corporation Deeds record that Spon Bridge, which denotes the boundary, was in existence in the late 13th century and by 1411 houses were built near it. This included a long stone building on the north side with an orchard called 'Le Cadelond.'

This early bridge must have fallen into disrepair for it is claimed that the present bridge (which looks mediaeval) once had a date inscribed on the keystone giving the date of its erection as 1771. Another temporary bridge reportedly stood here in 1767. Before this bridge was built a holloway led down to a ford and just below stood a narrow packhorse bridge, believed to have been built in 1616. Before the bridge was built it is recorded that when the Sherbourne was flooded stagecoaches waited at an inn in Allesley until the water subsided. One coach, the Liverpool coach in 1765, tried to cross the flooded ford and got trapped. Luckily all survived and one man is said to have undressed to swim to the bank.

It is often said that Spon Bridge was constructed from the remains of Spon Gate and the Coventry Cross, which were both demolished in 1771. However, there is evidence that the Coventry Cross actually stood for another few years. Some sources state that the pinnacles on the bridge, which once

An early 19th-century engraving of the Sherbourne Viaduct, which carried the London to Birmingham train before its collapse. (CCL)

Spon End, photographed in 1910, showing a converted barn and part of the Spon Viaduct. (CCL)

held lamps, may have come from the cross, although that seems unlikely. Much of the bridge was probably built from reused stone from the gate, some of which was also used to fill up the old holloway, which lay alongside the bridge. Another bridge, which stands inearby in the Butts, is a beautiful 50ft cast-iron bridge created in 1837 by C.B. Vignoles and cast at the ironworks at Turton. This handsome structure bridged an arm of the Oxford Canal, which used to run across Sowe Common, until 1969.

An article written in the *Coventry Times* in 1900 mentioned Spon End in 1800:

> *Spon End too, was rural in character, the land for the most part being Lammas* [land only opened from Lammas Day] *with here and there a barn standing thereon. Early in the century there is a record ... of a barn in Spon End being converted into dwelling houses. There was also a pinfold here* [a pound for stray animals by the arches] *... which in 1816 was rebuilt.*

This pinfold, like all others around the city, was built and maintained by the City Chamberlains, who pocketed the money taken in fines for stray animals.

On the night of 26 January 1857, during a particularly tempestuous night, the residents of Spon End were woken three times by thunderous crashes. Those who ventured out in the morning found that 23 arches of the Spon railway viaduct had collapsed, leaving only five standing. Thousands flocked to see the damage, with roads blocked and the Sherbourne diverted by the rubble. The viaduct, which was a quarter of a mile long, was completed in 1849 and made from sandstone taken

Houses below Spon Viaduct in 1947. The tallest building is the Black Horse, a popular Spon End pub since Georgian times.

from a quarry on Barrs Hill. The missing arches were rebuilt in brick in 1857 and the railway reopened in 1860. From the main road one can still see the original and replacement arches.

Four Pounds Avenue was originally a cinder track. In 1956 a dual carriageway was named after the four pound or mill pool, which impounded the water for a watermill known as Jordan's Mill. The mill stood on the site of the Renold Chain and its four ponds ran along the Spon End Valley from the present Four Pounds Avenue. It was written in 1883 that when the water mill was built the Sherbourne was diverted to higher ground.

In 1944 it was written that:

> ... the water for Jordan's Mill was impounded into a dam, and it was there, in the summer days long ago that boys and youths of the district used to enjoy a bathe in the waters, which were often deep enough to provide a really good 'dabble'.

Councillor Andrews also wrote of it: 'The Four Pound is also used by boys for bathing. I observed about thirty there on the afternoon of August 8th 1882.' The site of this mill pool is now overgrown and shrunken to a stream, but the waterfall that fed it can still be seen down a back track at the bottom of the Arches Industrial Estate.

The original bed of the Sherbourne continued to be fed mainly by springs and was called the Barley Brook. It was said in 1883 that the water was good except for contamination caused by cattle. On one occasion water from the Barley Brook was used for the whole city centre.

After the demolition of Jordan's Mill the Coventry Chain Company moved there in 1907 and produced chains of all types and sizes. The company was renamed Renold Chain in 1954 and closed in 1980.

A drawing by Florence Weston of Jordan's Mill, driven by the Sherbourne, as it looked in the 19th century. The water still runs here but nothing in the picture remains.

One of the best-known inns in Spon End still stands despite attempts to have it demolished for road widening. Men were supping ale in the Black Horse back in 1750. In 1818 it was kept by Mary Twigg and was said to be the centre of the court of Charles Lilley. Lilley was a director of the poor and very well respected. He frequented the Black Horse and, while his white horse and carriage waited outside, he would settle disputes. All knew Lilley as the 'King of Spon' and a saying developed: 'Go to Lilley, he will settle your arguments'.

Another long-gone inn, the Hare and Squirrel, was said by Hewitt in 1765 to be 'the first house on coming into the city.' Here in that year Hewitt arrested one Richard Swift, a notorious thief and highwayman, who had been tried at the Old Bailey five times and escaped the gallows in return for information. He was later transported to America for 14 years, bought his freedom and returned to England and within an hour of arriving in Coventry was arrested in Spon End by Alderman John Hewitt, Coventry's great thief-taker. Swift was tried at the April Assize and, much to the surprise of all, including his mistress who had brought money to bury him, was acquitted. Hewitt re-arrested him despite the court's decision and had him moved back to London, where he was convicted and transported again.

Further Reading
Newspapers, Local Studies.
Alderman John Hewitt, *Hewitt's Journals*, 1750s and 1760s.

STIVICHALL

The earliest spelling for Stivichall dates from around 1144 and is thought to come from the Old English '*styfic*' meaning stump and '*healh*' meaning an overgrown corner of land. There have been 14 different spellings for Stivichall, including Spichall, Stivichal, Stychill, Styvechall and of course the modern favourite Styvechale. The 'stump' may refer to an obvious landmark at the entrance to the original village, 'The Grove', a piece of raised land or stump containing a grove of trees.

The parish of Stivichall was bounded on the northeast by the fence and ditch of Cheylesmore Park, the historical estate of the Black Prince. Stivichall was first documented in the 12th century as one of the chapelries restored to Coventry Priory by Ranulf Gernon, Earl of Chester. A justice field was set aside so mortal combat could decide guilt or innocence. After Ranulf's death in 1153, his son Hugh Kevilok gave the manor, including its manor house, to Walter Durdent, Bishop of Coventry, for the absolution of soul of his father, whom Durdent had had excommunicated. The church held the manor until the 16th century.

In 1529 Thomas Gregory, a lawyer, arrived in Coventry to take up the post as town clerk. In 1538 he married Elizabeth Wade, daughter of the mayor, Christopher Wade, who held the manor house. Wade died in 1539 leaving the estate to his daughter and son-in-law. The estate transferred to his son Arthur on his death in 1574 and Arthur continued to consolidate the family holdings in Stivichall.

Another large landowner in Stivichall was the Ferrers family. In 1573 Arthur Gregory married into the family, thus merging the two estates. He acquired more land from Lord Berkeley in 1580. By the end of the century the Gregorys had acquired not only the whole parish of Stivichall, but also property in Coventry, Foleshill, Walsgrave, Brinklow, Canley, Kingshill, Finham, Stoneleigh and Weston-under-Wetherley. The parish also became a popular home to many of Coventry's elite, including the Swillington family. In 1552 Elizabeth Swillington, widow of Coventry's Recorder, gave the rentals of certain properties to maintain roads around the city, especially the road from Stivichall to Coventry.

The original manor house of the Gregorys is thought to have become Bremond College (No.28 Leamington Road). In 1755 Arthur Gregory began to build a new hall and in the process demolished the old village, leaving only the church, Stivichall Grange and a few other buildings standing in Stivichall hamlet. The existence of this estate stopped the expansion of Coventry into the district until the estate was sold in the 20th century.

The last of the Gregorys died in 1909 and the estate passed to a

Stivichall Hall as it appeared in 1936.

An early 19th-century painting showing the beginning of the Kenilworth Road, in front of Stivichall Common. The inn known as the White House was a popular meeting place for Coventry watchmakers who would often be seen sitting outside. (CCL)

cousin, Alexander Hood, who later adopted the surname Gregory-Hood. It was he who sold the land for the Memorial Park in 1922. Alexander died in 1927 and was succeeded by his son, Major Charles Hugh Gregory-Hood, who sold the estate to Coventry Corporation in 1928. The family moved to Loxley Hall, near Stratford. Stivichall Hall became derelict and was demolished after World War Two. The grounds and estate were built over in the 1960s and 70s.

The War Memorial Park came into being after the end of World War One when the Coventry War Memorial Committee approached Alexander Gregory-Hood to sell some of his land to establish a park to remember the dead. An agreement was made to sell 183 acres for £31,562 8s 9d, which was raised by public subscription. The land was formally handed over in 1920 and on 9 July 1921 the Memorial Park and an area of 122 acres were opened to the public.

The Corporation added to the park by creating a rock garden and ornamental gardens. There were also 44 tennis courts, three bowling greens and 19 football and hockey pitches. In the first six years 181 copper beeches were planted by Coventrians in memory of lost sons or fathers.

In November 1923 Coventry architects were invited to design a permanent monument to stand in the park. The competition was won by city architect T.F. Tickner. In 1924 a public appeal was made to raise £5,000 to build his design. The memorial was unveiled on Saturday 8 October 1927 by Field-Marshal Haig. The Bishop of Coventry dedicated the memorial to the 2,587 men of Coventry who gave their lives for king and country. Haig placed the roll of honour in an oak cabinet in the 'chamber of silence' inside the memorial. The memorial has been repeatedly vandalised by youngsters and in 2002 it was restored and protected against graffiti.

The Kenilworth Road, although first mentioned in 1313, is older than that and was the road from Coventry to Kenilworth which was cleared of vegetation by Simon de Montfort to stop highway robbery in the 12th century. At the junction of this and the old Warwick Road was the Grove, which was a grove of elms in the 17th century. The fact that it was a grove of trees may mean that it was an ancient sacred site and explain why a cross called the Queen's Cross once stood there. The beautiful tree-lined Kenilworth Road was created in the late 18th century by Lord Gregory. They were said to have been planted in anticipation of the future needs of the Navy, and for his patriotism Lord Gregory was rewarded with supporters for his coat of arms.

Of the original village little remains, not even the church. The original church of St James, thought to date from around 1270, was pulled down by Francis Gregory in around 1800 and replaced with the present edifice. Supposedly the church was built by one stonemason, James Green of Coventry, with the help of only one labourer. It opened in 1817, having taken seven years to complete. The only remains of the original church are a Norman font. The church continued to be used by the Gregorys, who had a drive to it from the hall.

Another interesting building, which is now flats, is Stivichall Grange, a beautiful 14th-century grange that belonged to Coventry Priory. In around 1920 it became the home of the Hollick family,

The smithy at Stivichall, photographed in around 1860. (CCL)

who farmed the land until the 1960s. In 1961 Mr R. Hollick, then aged 87, was interviewed by the *Coventry Evening Telegraph*, which reported:

> *From his 14th-century moated grange with its sunken lawn, aged fruit trees and mysterious shrubberies, Mr Hollick has watched the advance of an army of trim suburban villas surrounding the farm's perimeter. The land he farms forms part of 120 acres bought by a London firm for development as one of Coventry's biggest private housing schemes.*

Mr Hollick continued to fatten his cattle and told reporters that his father had been a magistrate and had farmed in Foleshill and at Stivichall Manor Farm, which is now Bremond College. He stated that before he went into semi-

Coventry's War Memorial in the War Memorial Park, unveiled in October 1927. (CCL)

Coat of Arms Bridge Road, with the Gregory bridge, photographed in 1870. (CCL)

Children on Stivichall Common in around 1912. One could say this area was the pleasure ground of Coventry.

retirement he was a well-known face at Coventry Cattle Market and local shows as a breeder of prize-winning Warwickshire Longhorns. The article continued:

> *Mr Hollick is one of the oldest surviving boys of King Henry VIII School … but now as the city encroaches on his preserves, Mr Hollick finds … he is kept too busy by that section of modern youth which apparently delights in damaging other peoples property. Broken glass in the orchard, fruit stealing and vandalism around his cattle sheds are among the trials he has to endure. He experienced vandalism of a different kind in 1940 when a parachute bomb blew up his greenhouse, but left untouched staddle stones by the dozen which still stand … and some old fashioned waggons and carts.*

By 1971 Mr Hollick had left the farm and the building had been vandalised. Colonel A.M.H. Gregory-Hood applied to have it demolished. Thankfully the main building was saved and still stands today, one of the finest mediaeval buildings in Coventry.

One building that did not survive the 1960s was the Stivichall tollgate house. This small building with its two gates controlled access to the road to Stoneleigh and the Kenilworth Road. Stagecoaches, carts and waggons rattled past it in the late 18th century.

In 1800 a weighing machine was added and vehicles above a certain weight were not allowed to use the road without paying extra, probably because of damage to the turnpike. The turnpike road was not always safe. In January 1776 a gentleman was stopped by two highwaymen, described as 'well mounted', who brandished their pistols and demanded money. The highwaymen were disturbed and rode off with only £15 but they continued to operate in the area. The *Coventry Mercury* of 1780 offered a reward for the apprehension of robbers who had accosted Richard Armstrong, landlord of the Salutation Inn, near the tollhouse. On 14 January 1793 the *Mercury* reported:

Rush Pit Cottages off the Kenilworth Road at Burnt Post, Stivichall, in around 1880.

On Friday night last, about seven o'clock, three daring villains stopped Mr Ridges, of Kenilworth, near Mr Benbow's, on Stivichall Common; they pulled him from his horse and one of the ruffians seized him by the throat and held him down while the other two rifled his pockets; they took from him three guineas in gold, some silver, and a metal watch. And some little time before, at or near the same place, another person was stopped and robbed by the same villains.

Ornamental gardens in the War Memorial Park in the 1930s. Beyond the Scots firs of 'The Grove' can be seen.

Coventry Great Fair in the War Memorial Park in 1953.

In 1818 an inquest into the death of William Law, aged 23, was held at the Windmill pub in Stivichall. An argument between a group of youths over a hat had escalated and Law was stabbed in the stomach by William Jackson. Law died the following morning and Jackson was put on trial for wilful murder. He was found guilty of manslaughter at the Warwick Assizes. The Windmill pub may be what was also known as the White House, a favoured meeting place for watchmakers, and a venue

An early 19th-century painting of Stivichall Tollgate. The open gate led onto the Kenilworth Road; beyond is 'The Grove', then covered with many more Scots firs than today. The other gate gave access to the church of St James and Stivichall Hall. (CCL)

for dancing, coursing and cockfighting, if the police were not close by.

In the latter part of the 19th century other incidents occurred in Stivichall. A policeman was shot and stabbed on the corner of Cabbage Square, and on the bend of the road Lord Leigh's coachman had the cockade shot out of his hat. The same gang pursued a local farmer to his house. Armed police officers retaliated by hiding in the trees below the tollgate to try to catch the criminals, but nothing happened that night or again afterwards.

In April 1837 two soldiers, Colonel McAlpine and Lieutenant Stock , fought a duel with pistols in a field near the tollgate. McAlpine had a lucky escape on the first shot when the button of his waistcoat was shot off. Both men missed in a second exchange of fire and they left the field with their honour intact.

Back in 1803 the tollgate keeper was summoned before the city magistrates for refusing to allow the 6th Regiment of Dragoons, stationed in Coventry Barracks, to pass through the gate without paying. This plucky individual was forced to hand back the cash he had received and promised not to repeat the offence.

The present hamlet of Stivichall, presented to the city in 1932 by Major Charles Hugh Gregory-Hood, is often thought of as the actual village. It was described by local historian Abe Jepcott:

Here was a pond with coloured ducks and moorhens swimming so near the road, a little half timbered cottage near the bridge, a punt on the pond, a sheep dip nearby and the blacksmith's forge to complete the pleasing picture.

As we munched our biscuits we looked at the blacksmith's shop, the door hung wide open and a horse was tied to a ring in the wall. The big bellows were blowing the forge fire up in bluey green and fierce red tongues of fire and the face of the blacksmith looked the colour of old port wine! He poked his giant pincers into the flames and brought out a white-hot horseshoe. The horseshoe was put on the anvil and the clang of a big hammer on it sent it into a thousand shooting sparks of silver and gold. We saw the blacksmith nailing a shoe on a horse but the smell of burning hoof nearly choked us, so we came out into the fresh air.

These buildings and others stood in Coat of Arms Bridge Road; originally called Cock's Lane it was renamed after the railway bridge was built by the London and North Western Railway for the Coventry to Kenilworth line in 1844. On the bridge are cut the arms of the Gregory-Hoods and the motto 'Vigilante'. Below this stood the old stone-built pinfold to hold straying cattle; some remains still exist after it was restored some 20 years ago.

The mediaeval Stivichall Grange standing semi-derelict in 1971.

The pool mentioned earlier fluctuated in size depending on the season and often spilled onto the road. It was later known as the White Rail Pit because it was partly hemmed in by white railings after a farm labourer drowned in the pool at night. It was located off the Kenilworth Road around its present junction with the Kenpas Highway. By the pool once stood an attractive huddle of thatched and timbered cottages called Burnt Post Cottages. These were part of a popular walk used by Coventrians and courting couples to take the air, known as the 'Monkey Parade.' Near the entrance to Stivichall Hall was a set of railings, which were tarred every Saturday to stop courting couples leaning on them and kissing!

The area in which the cottages stood was known simply as Burnt Post, a name which has caused speculation. The present Burnt Post pub on Kenpas Highway stands some distance from the original Burnt Post hamlet. The *Coventry Standard* of March 1854 tells of a gentleman being robbed and assaulted on the Kenilworth Road. His rider-less horse was stopped at the tollgate. The event took place at 'Bourne Post' not Burnt Post, so the name may have changed. There was once a stream crossing the road near this spot and it has been suggested that it was marked by a post, a bourne 'stream' post. This may have been a marker to show the depth in times of flood or have been to help people to cross. This explanation is backed up by a letter published in the *Coventry Standard* of 1958 when a Mrs Irene Morris stated that when she was young in the 19th century it was never called Burnt Post, but Burn Post. She recalled: 'the stream was narrow enough for me to jump across it, holding onto the post for support.' The Green Lane area was originally open land and farmland. In 1926 the Green Lane Estate was built under the jurisdiction of Warwick Rural District Council and during work a prehistoric battle-axe was found. By 1929 Coventry Corporation took over the estate and it was said that with the hidden costs they had bought a 'pig in a poke.' Improvements such as drainage and roadside kerbs were needed and the newly created Residents Association fought for them, as well as an improved gas supply and street lighting.

The estate was described in 1930 thus:

Walk through this avenue ... notice the forecourts of the houses with their plentiful chrysanthemums of all colours; notice the dainty treatment of the windows of the houses by the careful housewives, by their blinds and curtains ye shall know them; notice the brightness of the shopping centre; notice, in fact, the whole appearance of this, one of the newest of Coventry's suburbs.

Further Reading
Abe Jepcott, 'The Story of Coventry', *The Guildsmen Magazine*, 1969.
Victoria County History, Vol. 8.
Various newspaper cuttings, Local Studies.

STOKE

'*Stocca*', the word from which Stoke derives, appears to be Old English, meaning village. Some have suggested it may mean a special religious place. There is no known early history of Stoke but evidence of ancient activity in the area was found during house building in May 1938. The *Midland Daily Telegraph* reported that 'Local archaeologists attach considerable importance to the finding of a hand-axe of the Palaeolithic period which has been made in the Stoke district of Coventry on land which is at present being developed.'

Stoke was first mentioned as one of the chapelries given to Coventry Priory by Ranulf, Earl of Chester. It has been speculated that there was once a chapel here dedicated to St Chad. Blyth, in his *History of Stoke*, concludes that the original chapel from which the present church is derived was always dedicated to St Michael. However, there is a reference from 1557 that states, 'The saied long medowe to a well in the high way ou' agayn' stoke church called saynt Chadds Well.'

In 1279 the principal freeholders were the priory, Nicholas de Segrave, Thomas de Wiltshire, Robert de Stoke and Thomas de Adern. The Stoke family held land here as early as 1221 and by the 14th century they had built a manor house by the church. The family lived at the manor house, called Stoke Hall, until the 16th century.

In 1690 part of the boundary at Stoke Green was recorded as passing the 'Hermitage Barne; so up the Causway to the end thereof near Jabet Ash.' Jabet or Jabbet's Ash had a long history as a

Lathing big guns at the Ordnance Works in 1916. (CCL)

Part of the mediaeval Stoke tile kilns excavated during the building of Harefield Road. The two arches led into the fires, which baked the tiles, stacked in the chamber above.

boundary point and meeting place. The ash stood near the corner of the present Binley Road at the intersection with Marlborough Road. A deed over 600 years old from the reign of Richard II mentions 'Jabbotsashe', although even then it was an ancient landmark. There are many theories as to how it got its name. One states that it is named after Joybert, one time prior of Coventry. This is very unlikely, but the tree is sometimes referred to as the Gibbet Ash, which does make some sense. In the Saxon period ash trees were sacred to the god Woden and sacrifices would be made by hanging people, usually criminals, on ash trees. These trees later became known as Gibbet Ashes. The practice seems to have continued for judicial purposes for in 1183 a boundary charter of Hugh Kevilok, Earl of Chester, refers 'to Stoke, as far as the Gibbet.' The word Jabbet therefore seems to be a corruption of

the word Gibbet. Jabbet's Ash was the Gibbet Ash and until the mid-19th century a double-bank and ditch could still be seen by the tree, marking the ancient boundary.

In 1603 when Lord Harington of Coombe Abbey brought the Princess Elizabeth (daughter of James I) to Coventry for the first time, they were met by the mayor and commonalty

The Peel-Conner Telephone Works, later the GEC, photographed in 1922 in semi-rural Stoke. (CCL)

at the ash. Previously in 1470 Edward IV passed the tree on his way to Coombe Abbey. It appears that throughout its history Jabbet's Ash has been constantly replaced, the last being planted in 1925, from stock of its predecessor.

The Revd T.A. Blyth described the village in the 1890s as:

> ... most pleasantly situated ... From many parts of the parish very varied and pleasing views of the 'Three Spires' may be obtained. The roads generally are very good and the footpaths numerous. Some of the lanes are very pretty where ferns and wild flowers abound, and are much frequented by Coventry pedestrians, bicyclists and tri-cyclists. We have a considerable variety of song and other birds.
>
> Stoke is rich in Parish Gardens [allotments] ... They were formerly part of the Common, and were enclosed about 63 or 64 years ago ... Stoke Common consists of 66 acres. Stoke Heath is covered with gorse and green pasture. There is a level piece near the centre used as a Cricket ground. Stoke Green to the south of the heath, consists almost entirely of level turf. Here every year, during the season, a vast number of Cricket matches take place between local and other clubs.

In 1911 when ex-councillor Howells was developing the Harefield Estate between the Stoke Road and Walsgrave Road an unusual find was made. Stonework was revealed and the men uncovered the huge remains of a set of mediaeval tile kilns. Tiles found showed remains of green glaze and other tiles were of the encaustic inlaid type commonly found in churches from the 14th to the 16th century.

Close to the kiln several stone channels were discovered, which appeared to be the drains of a large house. The house was in fact the home of the master potter in charge of the tile kiln 'factory'. The owner of the house in the 16th century was one William Ruyley. In the Public Record Office in London a document records an incident here in the 16th century. It reads:

> At an inquest held at Stoke in the county of the city of Coventry, by John Boteler, coroner of the lord the king ... on Thursday next after the Feast of the Nativity of the Blessed Virgin Mary, the eighth year of the reign of King Henry VIII, twelve jurors said that, 'John Ruyley, and a certain Alice, servant of the aforesaid William Ruyley, at Stoke, about the ninth hour of the said day, standing together in the hall of the house of the said William Ruyley, called a tyle house, where tyles are made, in which house a certain William Besworth of Stoke, labourer, was making tiles; and he took in his hands a certain piece of clay from which he made a tile, and intended to throw that said piece of clay at the said Alice, it struck the said John Ruyley, on his left side, from which blow the said John languished for two days and died. And as soon as the said accident had been caused by the said William Besworth, he took to flight, the jurors know not wither. He has a sheep worth twelve pence, but he has no other goods.'

Tiles from the kilns graced most of the monastic buildings in the area and no doubt most of the homes of the well-to-do. The tilers also made roof tiles; in 1368 John de Coughton of Stoke was accused by Adam Keresley of failing to have 8,000 tiles ready.

Buildings on the Walsgrave Road suddenly ended at the junction of Bray and Clay lanes. Beyond lay fields until Church End and Stoke Church. All these houses were later converted into shops.

It appears that when tile making stopped in the 16th century clay pipe making began. One producer supplying the local area was G.H. Holt of Bray's Lane and Field Row. He was in production from around 1873 to 1915. Holt produced both plain pipes and decorated ones, showing the three spires and elephant and castle or Godiva.

In 1963 Mr A. Wallace of Clovelly Road spoke to a reporter from the *Coventry Standard* about his memories of Stoke Heath in Edwardian times. He remembered an old footpath to Stoke running from Hillfields:

The latter portion of the footpath was rather perilous at night as it ran alongside quite a sizeable ditch ... Barras Green, which was the nominal centre of this little outpost of the city, consisted of the Red Horse Inn and a few cottages ... Yet another path ran along what is now Mercer Avenue, through a swinging iron wicket gate at the bottom of Coventry Street. It passed the end of North Street [which boasted a variety of cottages and some weavers houses with top floor workshops, which still exist] *and ran towards what is now Stoke Heath School, with Stoke Common on one side of the path and fields on the other.*

This path continued through the avenue of trees still to be seen at the end of Mercer Avenue, and joined the paths running from the end of Blackberry Lane...On one side of this old footpath stood an old cottage. It had a sizeable garden and rather vulnerable plum trees. The cottage was inhabited for many years by an old lady, whose name I believe was Cooknell. She often stood by her garden gate sucking a clay pipe! Opposite this cottage was a huge sand pit, it has long since been filled in with refuse from the city and now accommodates a number of football pitches [Stoke Heath]. *This was used by some of the local youths as a venue for various illegal coin games and was reasonably secure from the arm of the law. On the far side, where now stands the Morris Engines factory* [Courthouse Green] *was a farm kept by a farmer named Jordan, and many happy hours I have spent here helping with haymaking.*

Stoke Row, with its cottages [one of which remains] *branched off and continued past the end of Stratford Street as a muddy lane, between large elms to the school. Then it went right, past a few more cottages and Boneham's Farm, to join Clay Lane, this at the time being a very true name. It was eventually made up and the first bus service from the city terminated at Barras Green. There, the solid-tyred open-topped, wooden seated buses turned around and picked up passengers for town, near what is now a butchers shop and before that a very large pond.*

Stratford Street contained many of the houses there today, but at the junction with Shakespeare Street stood a large orchard. From this it was possible for small boys to extract fruit, in spite of being under the watchful eye of the owners, who lived in a cottage opposite. The south end of Shakespeare Street terminated in a ditch, and this street also boasted an out-door beer shop; a cool place with stone floor and rows of barrels, and a slaughterhouse. It was quite a common thing for a pig or a cow to escape and chase around the district.

Milton Street had a small brick built Primitive Methodist Chapel ... and ended at a gate with a row of cottages on either side. The gate led to a delightful footpath across Stubb's Farm and through the meadows and over five stiles to Wyken Church. One field somewhere near where the Devonshire Arms now stands, boasted a sunny bank, upon which primroses and violets bloomed in profusion.

Stoke Common with open country around the village green, used to be the scene of much activity, winter and summer. I well remember quite good cricket matches being played there, and football in the winter. The home team I think was called 'Stoke Athletic', the dressing room was in the Red Horse. Here then were seven streets and a village green, a little self contained community, a mile away from the edge of the city and surrounded entirely by open country.

Stoke Green appears to have first become popular in the 17th century, when it was described as being full of summerhouses with a bowling alley past the orchard opposite Jabbet's Ash. One resident was Dr Samuel Hinton MA, son of William Hinton, vicar of St Michael's in Coventry. Hinton must have had royalist tendencies for in the period leading up to the English Civil War he wrote:

A grate rumor was spread yt I should be questioned for calling Mr Pim [John Pym, Parliamentary leader, held coal pits around Coventry], *a collier. The occasion was this; The summer before, when ye Parliament was broke off. I was in discourse at Stoke Green about assistance to bee given to ye Kinge against ye Scotts ... I did declare they would doe more for Pim ye Collier than for ye Kinge.*

Hinton had many problems during the war and was forced to leave Coventry. He took a house at Stoke Green before being moved on to Lichfield.

Stoke Rectory, home of the Revd T.A. Blyth, photographed in around 1906. (CCL)

Others residents of the Green were also influential people, such as William Partridge and Christopher Hall, both doctors, and Thomas Wagstaffe of Stoke Green Farm, who was described as a captain in Cromwell's time. In 1655 much of the common ground, referred to as 'Common Corn Fields', was enclosed. The enclosure award shows many names now lost, like Shugborough Grove,

Stoke National School in 1905, now the 'Academy' and still used for its original purpose. (CCL)

Jabbet's Ash, photographed before its removal and replanting in 1915. (CCL.)

Lamp Lands, Parson's Meadow, Gulson's Piece, Lake Furlong, Cockpit Corner and Gallow Furlong by Jabbet's Ash. Among these enclosures cottagers set up home. According to the *Victoria County History* Binley Road dates from this period. The building known as The Langleys is said to have 17th-century origins.

In the 18th century horseracing took place at Stoke, referred to as 'Stoke Race' in 1772. In 1830 the races came back to Stoke before moving to Radford in 1852. The site of the mile-long racetrack was said to lie between Gosford Green and the present Marlborough Road (other sources state that it lay in the present circular estate of Stoke Park). In 1835 the Craven Trial Stakes were run here and quality horses ran as the course was considered a trial course for the Derby. No horse that ran here actually won the Derby, the nearest was Fitzroy, beaten in his next race by Coronation, winner of the 1841 Derby. At Stoke races on 4 March 1834 the first race took place at 12pm followed by races every half-hour, except the race for a 100oz silver cup. A meal for the winners was held in Coventry at the King's Head Hotel.

After this particular race a piece appeared in the *Coventry Herald* stating:

> *The Stoke races may now be considered fairly established as a festival of the sporting calendar. From the experience of Tuesday last, we feel justified in this conclusion. The 'arrivals' of Monday led us to anticipate a good day to follow. The 'bog-trotters'* [country people] *were on the move early in the morning; and the prigs* [thieves] *and beaks* [police] *were looking with a jealous eye on each other, waiting for business; of which, however owing to the vigilance of the latter, there was fortunately little done. During the morning visitors of all classes were arriving in great numbers, and intense interest was excited. By twelve o'clock a larger concourse of people had assembled than we ever remember to have witnessed in the vicinity of Coventry, supposed to amount to 10,000 including many distinguished personages and gentry of the county, and sporting characters of the celebrity.*

Unsavoury characters also lived locally. In November 1772 Alderman John Hewitt, Coventry's mayor and thief-taker, issued this notice in the *Coventry Mercury*:

> *A ROBBERY AND MURDER – Whereas on the Third of November 1772, between the hours of one and three o'clock in the night, three men came to the turnpike house, near Binley Bridge, and forcibly broke into the same, and one of them by discharging a loaded pistol, wounded the keeper of the said gate, (of which wound he is since dead) and afterwards plundered his house of ten pounds and upwards, about seven shillings …*

The tollgate, although called the Binley Tollgate, stood within the boundary of Stoke, the River Sowe at nearby Binley Bridge being the actual boundary. The tollhouse stood just above the present junction of the Binley Road and Hipswell Highway. In those days it was a narrow lane, with a well opposite the tollhouse, which is now under the busy dual carriageway.

The men who robbed the tollgate were Thomas Farn and John Howe, both of Brinklow. On the night of the incident they slowly rode through the tollgate while Charles Pinchbeck, the keeper, was

Church Lane in Stoke looking north towards the Walsgrave Road, photographed in 1911. Note the weaver's cottage with its top shop. (CCL)

asleep. They crossed Binley Bridge and dismounted in a field. Here Farn tested and loaded his pistol. Back at the tollhouse Farn removed a windowpane and entered. Unable to get any further in the house he climbed back out and went to the bedroom window where Charles Pinchbeck slept.

While Howe was uneasily walking away Farn banged on the window and Pinchbeck, half asleep, opened it, only to find he was facing a pistol. He grabbed at it and was shot through the hand. Farn reloaded and threatened to shoot him again if he didn't let him in. Pinchbeck did as he was told and Farn entered and stole the tollhouse takings.

Pinchbeck died of his injury and Alderman Hewitt started a murder hunt. He issued the notice in the newspaper and offered £90 for information. He received an anonymous letter naming Farn and Howe and connecting them with other crimes. The two were arrested and each blamed the other for the crime. In July 1773 they were put on trial and found guilty of the murder and robbery of Charles Pinchbeck. Four days later they were taken on a cart to the common ground above the tollgate and there they were hanged before a large audience. To their annoyance Thomas Wyat, a notorious receiver who first led them into crime, was among the crowd. After the bodies had hung for some time they were taken back to Coventry and delivered to the surgeons for dissection.

Despite the execution another robbery is recorded in January 1778 between the tollgate and the hilltop. Hewitt writes:

> *Thomas Bucknall was attacked by a person mounted on a bay mare, or gelding, with a pistol in one hand, demanded his money; upon this informants saying he had little, the highwayman immediately replied he would not be trifled with, as he knew he had twenty seven guineas: upon which this informant, apprehending his life to*

Men leaving the Humber Works in 1912.

be in danger, delivered his purse ... and the robber rode off towards Binley.

The well-known stocks at Stoke Green, next to the Bull's Head, are said by Blyth to have been erected around 1848–50. He claims they were built for William Kimberley. It appears Kimberley got drunk in the Bull's Head and caused a disturbance. He was fined and told that if the fine was not paid he would be placed in the stocks for six hours. He refused to pay and William Woodward built the stocks to hold him, but when they were completed he paid up. The only person actually placed in the stocks was a man named Hunt, another drunk. This story may not be true, as other sources claim the stocks date back to 1610. In 1998 the dilapidated original stocks were replaced with a copy. Below them once stood a pound in which stray animals were kept.

The area known as Stoke Park was developed from the 1860s and is completely surrounded by a curving sandstone wall. It is interesting that some sources suggest that this is the site of the old racecourse, because the shape of the wall does resemble the shape of a racecourse. The first house

An open-topped double-decker Maudsley bus travelling down the Walsgrave Road in 1914. The view remains the same except for the traffic. (CCL)

145

A drawing from the 1860s of Copsewood House off the Binley Road. This building was rebuilt and renamed Copsewood Grange. (CCL)

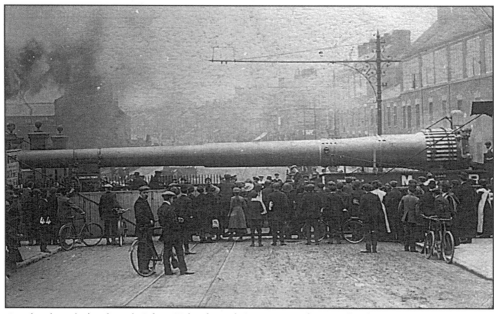

A naval gun being taken by rail from the Ordnance Works and across the Stoney Stanton Road in 1914. (CCL)

The remains of Biggin Hall and chapel from an early 19th-century painting.

built in the park was Park Cottage, erected by a builder called Malt in the Tudor style and containing salvaged material from many ancient buildings.

Leading towards the original village of Stoke is Ball Hill, originally called Stoke Knob, the 'knob' of course being the hill. In the 19th century the area, known simply as The Ball, is recorded as being steep and was a dirt track made up with stone and slag. It is believed the current name of Ball Hill was derived from the Ball Hill Hotel. In 1918 Ball Hill was just a row of private houses, ending by Clay Lane (then Clay Gate Lane) and overlooking open fields until it reached the original village by the church of St Michael, known as Church End. It appears that one of the houses was turned into a shop, followed by another, until the whole street formed the present shopping area of Ball Hill.

In 1861 around half of the population of Stoke (1,600 people) depended on weaving for their income. These were nearly all individual weavers with looms in top shops or sheds. With the collapse of weaving in 1860 and the decline in watchmaking and the closure of some local coal mines, there was much distress in Stoke. The population rose further after 1881 because of the development of Stoke as a suburb. In 1908 Humber opened their new factory in Humber Road (formerly Folly Lane). Here the company produced motor cars, cycles and motorcycles. After 1910 aeroplanes such as the Humber Monoplane were built based on Blériot's plane which first flew the English Channel in 1909. These were the first aeroplanes built in Coventry. In the 1930s the company built the famous Humber Snipe and the Pullman Limousine. During World War Two the company produced army vehicles, including Field-Marshal Montgomery's staff car. In the early 1960s the company was taken over by the Rootes Group and the last vehicle to bear the Humber name rolled off the track in 1976. Rootes eventually became Chrysler, which was itself taken over in 1978 by Peugeot-Talbot. The

The massive Rootes car factory (formerly the Humber) in Stoke and Stoke Aldermoor. (CCL)

factory site, which stretched over to Stoke Aldermoor, was also the birthplace of the Hillman, for it was here that William Hillman first built cars in a factory in the grounds of his mansion at Stoke Aldermoor. Formerly known simply as Aldermoor, this area consisted of farmland with farms such as Middleton's Farm, and a narrow lane with high hedge banks led to a group of cottages on the Aldermoor. Halfway down the lane, where there is now a pub, was a large pool, said to have been second to Quinton Pool for ice-skating in the winter.

Up to and after World War One industry moved into the Stoke district. This went hand-in-hand with house building centred around Stoney Stanton Road and Red Lane, a district that had had a number of cottages and villas since the late 19th century. The Ordnance Works in Red Lane caused house building at Stoke Heath in 1915 to house the workers. The Coventry Ordnance Works was built upon the site of Turrell's Farm and initially took over an old cycle component works, which had been there since the 1890s. In 1900 the company was placed on the Admiralty and War Office list and began to manufacture ordnance, but disappeared in the middle of the following year. It was then taken over by H.H. Mulliner, a carriage builder, and in 1903 was sold to Charles Cammell & Co. The making of ordnance for the military and Navy restarted. In 1906 it became the Coventry Ordnance Works Ltd and began producing field guns, huge naval guns (capable of shooting a 16in shell 22 miles), shells, torpedoes and ammunition trailers. A railway ran through the plant and carried everything including the naval guns across Stoney Stanton Road to the LNWR line. Marguerite Thorn recalled in 1981 that 'outside the naval shop, near Swan Lane, was an immense cast-iron firing pit for testing the guns before despatch. When this was in operation it could be heard all over Stoke and Foleshill and further.'

During World War One half of the factory produced shells. In *Red Lane Reminiscences*, Florence Jackson recalled the dangers: 'They used to fill the shell bodies with powder and often one blew up.' Florence Davis remembered 'There were two bad accidents there due to someone smoking. I think five were killed the first time and two the second.' Nelly Shirley added, 'My mother worked there at the fuse factory. She used to come home with all this yellow stuff over her.' This was Tetrol, the same explosive that stained the girls at White & Poppe in Whitmore Park. The factory was sold in 1922 and taken over by the Royal Navy in 1938 to manufacture and restore guns. After the war it was used as a naval depot and was closed in the mid-1970s, becoming an industrial estate.

In 1923 the telephone works (the GEC) began to be built at Copsewood Grange (a large Victorian mansion built in 1872). Alongside the works houses were built for the employees including a row of better-class houses facing a green on the Binley Road called Copsewood Terrace. These were for managerial staff. By World War Two much of the area was residential.

One section of Stoke which is largely forgotten is Biggin. The name is variously written as Bigging, Bygging or Bugging, and is said to be a Scandinavian word meaning a habitation or building. Forgotten Biggin, unlike most of the districts of Coventry, is actually mentioned in the Domesday Book. It has two entries under land held by Thorkil. From him Wulfric held one hide in Biggin with one plough, two villeins, one boarder and one slave. Another hide was held from Thorkil by Ralph, who had one boarder. It was held before the conquest by the Saxon Wulfstan.

The present Biggin Hall Hotel (built 1923) stands 430 yards southwest of the original moated Biggin Hall (which stood near the junction of Biggin Hall Crescent and Lindley Road). It is said that

Looking up Clay Lane in Stoke before World War One. The lane took its name from the fact that it was clay underfoot and very muddy in the winter.

Ball Hill, also known as Stoke Knob, on the Walsgrave Road in the 1920s. On the left stands the Old Ball Hotel, said to be near the site where King Richard planted his tent for the duel on Gosford Green.

in 1280 the prior of Coventry was the owner of the manor of Biggin. After the Dissolution the manor was granted to Coventry Corporation. In 1655 the tenant of Biggin Hall was William Partridge, 'Doctor of Physick'. In 1766 the hall belonged to the Draper's Company and they were still described as lords of the manor in 1923. The hall was let that year to Samuel Carter, a farmer. In 1818 part of the manor house was being used as a Sunday school and the rent was paid by Jonathan Bray, farmer of Biggin. In 1840 the house was occupied by James Duggins.

In around 1819 a gentleman by the name of George Sharp was born at the manor house. He informed the Revd Blyth that in his younger days, Biggin Hall was a large stuccoed house made into two, and that the remains of the old 'Roman Chapel' were made of stone. In the 19th century the building was still in use as a farm and remains of the ancient chapel could still be seen built into the building on the right. This was all that remained of the ancient hamlet and manor house of Biggin. All that survived in 1923 was part of the moat and some stonework. Housing was built and now not a trace survives.

Further Reading
Victoria County History, Vol. 8.
The Journal of Alderman John Hewitt.
Revd T.A. Blyth, *The History of Stoke*, 1897.
Red Lane Old Residents Association, *Red Lane Reminiscences*, 1983.
Various newscuttings, Local Studies.

The Bell Inn, Tile Hill, in around 1904. (CCL)

TILE HILL

Tile Hill was called 'Tylhul' in the 13th century, possibly taking its name from a mediaeval tile making site. The area lies beyond Fletchamstead and consists of some of the highest land in the Coventry area, more than 425ft up in Banner Lane, dropping to 365ft at the junction of Broad Lane and the Highway.

The area appears to have many connections with the Civil War. Banner Lane is said to have taken its name from the local tradition that Cromwell raised his banner here (on the site of Wickmans) before his troops attacked Kenilworth Castle. The story says that after marching down Cromwell Lane and turning into Red Lane the troops came across royalists and many were put to the sword. Blood ran everywhere and thus Red Lane got its name. Raising a banner this far from the castle seems strange, but if an army is straggling then to stop and gather them before reaching their destination does make military sense. Kenilworth actually came into the hands of the parliamentarians at the beginning of the war, so this could refer to an initial attack or troops heading for the

This photograph, taken in 1961, shows the Warwickshire Reformatory in Tile Hill Lane shortly before its demolition. (CCL)

151

parliamentarian held castle. To avoid the cost of garrisoning the castle it was slighted in 1648 and given to Colonel Hawkesworth, who continued its destruction.

Tile Hill also has Cromwell Cottage, where local tradition claims Cromwell spent the night and hid in the huge brick chimney. The cottage is certainly old and has a date on the porch of 1653. The

Tile Hill station and level crossing, photographed in 1931. (CCL)

timbered building may mostly date from that time, but the surviving stone-mullioned windows suggest that it originally dates from the 16th century. Cromwell was not in the district in 1653, but he was in Coventry in August 1651. Stories concerning Cromwell occur across the country, so who knows, maybe Cromwell passed by and a cottager offered him a drink of ale and the story grew. Local traditions should never be totally dismissed for there is nearly always a grain of truth in them.

For many centuries Tile Hill, like its surrounds, was part of the Stoneleigh Estate of Lord Leigh, until in 1926 Coventry Corporation acquired the land. Plants Hill Wood, running from Tile Hill Lane, is 24 acres of mixed woodland containing oaks up to 160 years old and beeches dating back 180 years. Pig Wood takes its name from the woodlands' ancient use of 'pannage', letting pigs loose in the oak wood and shaking down the acorns for feed. The Domesday Book records that there were 2,000 pigs on the Stoneleigh manor.

Limbrick Wood takes it name from the now gone Limbrick Farm. The area was originally called 'lingbok' and the name is said to come from the Celtic '*lyn*' meaning watercourse and '*cain*' meaning clear, hence the clear brook. The last major woodland in Tile Hill is Tile Hill Wood, covering over 72 acres; this was made a nature reserve in 1930.

Around the woodlands a small community lay scattered around the area in Tile Hill and down Banner Lane (the lower part is now called Cromwell Lane) to Burton Green. *Coventry Standard* reporter Brian Devine wrote in 1960:

By now everyone in and around Coventry is used to building projects … But perhaps the Broad Lane district is one which causes some surprise and occasionally resentment, when one thinks just how quickly this huge tract of land has been changed … About 50 years ago Broad Lane was a lane in the full sense of the word. After passing through the gates, which stopped the cattle straying on to Hearsall

Flats being built in Tile Hill in 1955–56. In the background can be seen the huge Tile Hill Wood. This scheme later won a Government award and was for many years considered one of the city's prime estates.

Common one could walk for miles along the lane where there was scarcely a house.

One person who lived right at the bottom of Broad Lane on the corner of Hockley Lane was 72-year-old Harriet Curtis. She was born in one of the old cottages that stood on the corner of the lane and remembered when the area resembled a 'Constable landscape.' Brian Devine continued:

> When Mrs Curtis was a girl, Broad Lane was the agricultural fringe of the city. Farmer's wives plodded all the way to Coventry to shop in all kinds of weather. Cattle grazing right up to the gates of Hearsall Common were common sights then. 'I remember my parents telling me that when they were young the people used to dance in the streets ... but of course there were no cars about in those days.' For the young children of that time one of the highlights of their day was to go up the lane and watch the old blacksmith [Duggin's Lane] shoeing horses.

The reporter then visited Harriet's neighbours, the Turners, in their 300-year-old cottage. Mrs Turner said, 'When we first came here there were only about a dozen houses between here and Coventry.' Her husband, then 72, had in the past used the front room to ply his trade as a cordwainer, and before that it was a sweet shop.

The railway came to rural Tile Hill in 1850 and the station was called Allesley Lane Station, changed in 1857 to Allesley Gate. Although not in the parish of Allesley, the district came under the parish councils of Allesley, Berkswell and Stoneleigh. It is said that when George V and Queen Mary visited Coventry the royal train pulled into a railway cutting here overnight and the following morning they could both be seen gathering wildflowers along the banks.

One of the most significant centres of employment in Tile Hill until recently was Massey-Ferguson tractors. The Banner Lane plant covered 1.8 million square feet, making it the largest tractor factory in the western world. The company was originally set up by Irishman Harry Ferguson, who designed a tractor that could literally grip the ground, transferring the pressure into the plough. In 1946 Ferguson made an agreement with the Standard Motor Company, which also built cars here for many years, to use their wartime shadow factory in Banner Lane. In 1953 Ferguson merged with Massey Harris of Canada and the company became Massey-Ferguson in 1958. The first tractor, the TE20, affectionately known as the 'Little Grey Fergie', was produced here, with 50,000 of them made, and altogether three million tractors were built at this plant. Currently there are believed to be over one million Massey-Ferguson tractors still working around the world. The company has recently fallen on hard times and production will soon cease. The company cannot compete with foreign makes and does not build the now more favoured giant tractor.

Further Reading
Mary Dormer Harris, *Some Manors, Churches and Villages of Warwickshire*.
Women's Institute, *The West Midlands Village Book*, 1989.
The Woodlands of Tile Hill, Coventry Leisure Services leaflet.

WALSGRAVE ON SOWE

The name means 'Wal's grave, or grove, by the Sowe'. Walsgrave was anciently known simply as Sow or Sowa and the later change to Walsgrave may indicate an ancient burial mound or sacred grove that once stood near the river. The district's ancient history is unknown, although there have been odd finds, including worked flints and a green quartz Neolithic hand-axe found near the river in the late 19th century.

Roman finds have been made around Walsgrave and Mount Nod is a name usually associated with Roman sites. In the Walsgrave triangle beyond Mount Nod evidence of a farm or small Roman villa was discovered when the Showcase cinema was built.

In the Cartulary of Coventry Priory it was claimed that 'Sow' had been held by the church since the reign of King Edgar, who died in 975. According to a later forged charter, in the reign of Edward the Confessor part of the village was given to the monastery of St Mary, Coventry, by Leofric and Godiva. In the Domesday Book it is recorded that the church held 3½ hides, with land for five ploughs. In the demesne were one plough and four slaves and 10 villeins with five ploughs. There was also a mill worth two shillings, and woodland half a league long.

The church of Coventry held the chapel here and the tithes of the manor. It also had a manor house, court leet, gallows, pillory, ducking stool, and the right to punish for breaking the laws on bread and beer. The prior's tenants from Walsgrave, Binley, Willenhall and Ryton attended the court leet here. This portion of the manor was held by Alexander Lapworth in 1604, whose grandfather had acquired it from Sir John Harington of Coombe Abbey.

The centre of Walsgrave village looking from Woodway Lane and up Hall Lane in around 1910. The building up the lane on the right is the Shoulder of Mutton pub. The children stand by the site of the later war memorial. (CCL.)

Walsgrave Hall, also known as 'Magpie Hall' because it was black and white, photographed when derelict, probably in the early 1950s. (CCL)

The second owner of Sowe, as recorded in the Domesday Book, was Richard the Huntsman, who held from the King one hide, land for 3½ ploughs, meadow and woodland three leagues long and one broad, which he shared with the King and the abbot of Coventry. The previous owner of the land before the Conquest was Colbrand.

Another early landowner here was one William de Crock. He committed a felony and his land was confiscated by the Crown. He was hanged and his land was passed on by Edward I (1272–1307) to the de Loges. Five tenements were held by Hugh de Loges from the Earl of Chester on condition that de Loges conducted:

> ... *the said Earl towards the King's Court, through the midst of the Forest of Tanck ... In the forest the Earl, might, if he pleased, kill one deer in his going and another on his coming back; giving unto Loges, at each time he should so attend him, a barbed arrow.*

In the time of Henry III (1216–1272) Hugh de Loges granted to William Bagot all his land in Sow to hold for the annual peppercorn rent of a pair of white gloves worth one penny, or one penny in money. This did not last, for the agreement was annulled when Richard de Loges proved his father was insane at the time of the agreement. Thus recovered the estate was settled on the widow of

Richard de Loges on condition that she presented a barbed arrow (some sources say a silver arrow) to the King whenever he should pass through Sowe on his way to Wales.

The village of Sowa became known as Sowe and in 1695 it is referred to for the first time as Walsgrave-on-Sowe. The pre-Domesday village appears to have stood between St Mary's church and the river Sowe, the site of the Domesday watermill. At some unknown period the original village was deserted and moved to higher ground. Until it was built upon in the 1960s the original settlement could still be seen, consisting of bumps, hollows and a dried-up moat. The site was probably changed because of plague, or flooding.

The original moated manor house appears to have stood close to the river, around the site of the hospital's staff accomodation. The later hall, first mentioned in 1559, stood on the site of Cloister Croft. Its owners included the Peyto and possibly the Lapworth families, then it came to William Wale in the 18th century. After his death in 1781 the estate passed to William Brown, Wale's daughter's husband. Brown rebuilt the hall in 1823 with 22 rooms.

In 1860 the estate passed to John Brown Izon and remained in his family until the 1890s when it was sold to William Wakefield, an oil magnate who lived there until 1952 when it was sold and converted into flats. The hall was sold again in 1962 and demolished, part of its grounds becoming the site of Walsgrave Hospital.

Walsgrave had a second manor house, probably connected to Richard the Huntsman's part of the manor. This large timbered building, known as Magpie Hall, stood on high ground opposite the Baptist Church. Magpie Hall is first mentioned in a lease granted from the Crown to Edward Lapworth in 1590. From this time until the 17th century it was the country residence of the Peyto family. By 1843 the building had been divided into cottages and in 1950 it was demolished. The land was empty until work began on houses and flats in 2002.

Walsgrave is connected to the earliest recorded trial for witchcraft in the country. In 1324 Richard de Sowe was murdered using sorcery. The murderer, John de Nottingham, had put a leaden pin through the head of an image of Sowe and the following day sent his servant to Walsgrave to check its effect. He found Sowe in a state of madness, unable to recognise anyone and crying 'Harrow'. Sowe was left like this for several days then de Nottingham pushed the pin into his heart, killing him within a few hours (see Shortley).

Walsgrave church has had many interesting vicars, including George Dale, who in 1642 was captured by parliamentary troops and 'led ridiculously' around Coventry. A new vicar, the Revd Frederick D. Perkins, arrived in the village on foot as darkness fell one night in 1817. Much to his bemusement not a soul could be found, but in the distance he could hear voices and see a hazy glare. He quickly made his way towards the light and to his horror found the entire village stood in a circle with men carrying blazing torches. In the centre of the circle was a bull tied to a stake. Two old women holding bulldogs fought one another to be first to release their animal against the unfortunate bull. Intending to inform the curate of the dreadful scene, Perkins pushed his way through the frenzied mob and strode to the nearby vicarage gates, where he was informed that the curate, Jones, had instigated the whole affair.

'John Brown's Cottage,' which stood in Potters Green. John Brown was a 19th-century carrier whose strong beliefs and oratorical skills led him into conflict with the vicar of St Mary's. When his child died unbaptised the vicar refused to bury him in the churchyard and so John buried his own child in an adjoining field. Many joined him at the burial and as a direct result of this incident national law was changed, giving everyone the right to burial in their local churchyard. (CCL)

Perkins informed Jones that he had come to replace him, and Jones ordered that the bull be placed in the vicarage stable. The following day Perkins gave Jones six weeks notice to vacate the vicarage. Six weeks later, having had no reply to letters to Jones, Perkins arrived in Walsgrave to find the vicarage doors and windows barricaded. He obtained an eviction order from the Sheriff of Warwick, but Jones nevertheless barricaded himself in the kitchen. Jones claimed that the order was invalid, as the front of the vicarage was in the county of Warwick and the back in the city and county of Coventry. Perkins went to Coventry to get an order and returned to find the vicarage empty but with all its windows smashed, either by Jones, or by villagers sad to lose their sporting curate. Perkins, however, went on to become the village's most eminent vicar, staying for 39 years.

The Craven Colliery, photographed before its closure after the General Strike of 1926. (CCL)

It is said of one 20th century vicar that he was fond of his drink

This beautiful cast-iron bridge now stands over the Sowe in The Butts; here it can be seen on its original site across a canal arm, which once crossed Sowe Common in Woodway Lane. (CCL)

and during his service would leave the church for a quick draught at the pub, using a gate he had made between the church and the Red Lion. When he left the vicarage it took many days to clear out the empty bottles.

Potters Green first appears as 'le Pottergrene' in 1411. It probably takes its name from a mediaeval potter's kiln. Originally a tiny hamlet in Woodway Lane (Wodeweye, 1350), it did not develop but remained a scattering of cottages leading up to Sowe Common (boscus de Sohe, 1203) until the 20th century.

In the summer of 1816 a member of the Congregation Chapel in Vicar Lane, Coventry, visited the area. He came on Sunday, hoping to preach to the inhabitants, whom he found 'in an heathenish state.' He talked all day long and as he was leaving a group of local urchins asked him if someone from his chapel would teach them to read and write, like other children. The result of this was the establishment of a Sunday school in the village, which also attracted adults and led to the opening of a chapel in 1820.

It appears that the inhabitants of Walsgrave were also fairly heathen, for the first Methodist and Baptist preachers were met with violence, being stoned by men, women and children. In 1835 Baptist minister Jabez Tunnicliffe tried again to establish the faith in the village. This met with much opposition, so much so that on one occasion a man was paid one sovereign to throw him down a well. However the man charged with the task fell into a drunken sleep in one of the local pubs and never accomplished his aim. The first Baptist chapel was eventually built in 1840. Those who lived in Potters Green referred to it as 'up the common', seeing themselves as independent from Walsgrave. Celebrations held there never went beyond the old Co-op building opposite Henley Road.

Walsgrave and Potters Green, like much of Wyken, depended on the local collieries, especially the Craven (off Deedmore Road) and Alexandra (off Shilton Lane). There was a scattering of weavers

Looking up Clifford Bridge Road as it passes through Walsgrave village in around 1910. The building on the right is the original Red Lion Inn and behind it stands St Mary's. All of the buildings on the left were demolished in the 1960s when the road was made into a dual carriageway.

in the village, and limited employment in agriculture. In the 19th century the local mines took on women and children; in the 1841 census William Ellis, aged eight, is listed as a miner. In 1851 Martha Jacques, aged eight worked a handloom at home. This was out-working for Coventry silk merchants, who sent men around local villages every week to collect the completed items. During the Great Strike of 1926 local villages were hit hard and men from Walsgrave earned a few coppers by doing work at Coombe Abbey. They gathered at the kitchen door for scraps and dripping. Many supplemented their family's diets with rabbits and pheasants illegally taken on the estate. After the strike some miners went to Binley, while the rest did other jobs or never worked again. Agriculture supplied one of the highlights of the year – hundreds gathered to see sheep being dipped by the High Bridge. The late Percy Collins recalled in 1986: 'They used to put 'em in the pens, used to drop 'em in arse back'ards in the water and then used to put the floodgates down in the brook and let the water run through a pipe into the wash pit.'

The village of Walsgrave did not really begin to develop until the 1950s. More housing was built around the village, and the Beckbury Road area was created from 1960. Ten acres of the land was once home to the Verrall sisters, Miss Florence and Miss Nee, who lived there from 1899 with their chauffeur, George Adams, and servants. Miss Nee is quoted as saying, 'People can't keep their servants these days, but ours don't want to go. They are perfect dears, all of them.' The sisters were perfect Edwardian ladies, one interested in hunting and riding and the other in the church and village school. All in the village doffed their caps or curtsied to the sisters if they met in the lanes. Things gradually changed and Miss Florence once said to the late Reg Johnson, 'Johnson, why don't you raise your hat

The church of St Mary the Virgin in Walsgrave.

to a lady, your father always did?' Miss Florence was shocked by the modern world and died in 1953 aged 93, followed eight months later by Miss Nee.

Walsgrave was one of the few local villages to have a yearly wake called Sowe Wake. Wakes developed from church vigils on the church's dedication day. Walsgrave's was always the first Sunday after 19 September and was held in the orchard of the Red Lion. There would be hand-driven roundabouts, darts, swing-boats, a fancy dress procession and singing and the local pubs opened all day. A traditional Sowe Wake fruit pudding was sold. The wake is believed to have stopped by 1910 and was later replaced by a flower show, which developed into the popular Walsgrave Show, an agricultural show eventually held in the grounds of Walsgrave Hall. It later combined with the Kenilworth Show and lives on at Stoneleigh.

Walsgrave in the late 20th century was one of the fastest growing areas in Coventry with the Walsgrave Triangle at its heart. Much of the development was on land owned by the Hall brothers, a name to conjure with in this part of the city. Few could now imagine the pleasant country lane that became the Ansty/Hinckley Road dual carriageway in the 1960s.

Further Reading
Sir William Dugdale, *Warwickshire*, 1817.
The Walsgrave Community History Project, *Walsgrave Chronicles*.
The Walsgrave Community History Project, *Walsgrave Remembered*, 1987.

WESTWOOD HEATH

Simply meaning 'the west wood on the heath', the district of Westwood Heath is still semi-rural. In the 12th century Henry II gave land here to the monks of Stoneleigh Abbey. It is said that when the Cistercians first came to the area in the 1150s they established a grange farm, which seemed to exist mainly to exploit the surrounding woodland. Opposite the site of what is generally thought to be the original Bockidene Grange in the present woodland called the Pools they dug their fish ponds, traces of which can still be seen. Remnants of the large woodland that once covered the area include Whitefield Coppice, Broadwells Wood, the Pools and the Black Waste Wood, once the Black West Wood.

The grange moat was over 30ft wide and kept the fish ponds full of water. There were once two buildings of uncertain age inside the moat, but the large size of the site and the lack of archaeological evidence of habitation has led some to suggest that it was a moated orchard or rabbit warren. There was once a hamlet here, for in 1325 the abbot of Stoneleigh forced 25 of his tenants to abandon their homes. Nearby Hurst and Cryfield were also affected. Hurst, once described as a pretty village, consisted of only one house in the late 15th century.

It is thought that the monks stopped using the site by the end of the 14th century and leased it. Experts believe that Bockendon Grange Farm, surrounded by a smaller moat, may have been the original grange farm. Although the present building dates back to the 18th century there are possible traces of mediaeval work. Behind Bockendon Grange Farm is another small moat that appears to have been created over ridge-and-furrow near the original settlement site. Further down the lane is the site of what is thought to be the lost village of Hurst.

Burton Green village school as seen in 2003. Note the 200-year-old oak growing through the fence.

Over the centuries the woodland that made up the area was cut down, creating open heath. This was enclosed in the late 18th and early 19th century to form farmland that still exists. The village of Westwood Heath began at Kirby Corner around a small group of cottages in the 19th century. Beyond them, in what

The Church of St John the Baptist, Westwood Heath, built in 1844 as a chapel to Stoneleigh parish.

is now Corner Road, stood a small smithy, then a track led to a saw mill. Beyond the saw mill stood the church of St John the Baptist, opened in 1844. A church booklet explains that for half a century the seating arrangements in the church remained the same:

> *The front seats were occupied by farmers and their families. Then came the middle seats for the craftsmen of the village; thirdly the agricultural labourers in the rear. This segregation was accepted ... Occasionally stray visitors came early to the morning service and unwittingly entered a front seat. To their consternation they were hauled out by the sexton and were conducted to a lower seat.*

The foundation stone was laid by Chandos, Baron Leigh, and the first incumbent was the Revd Edmund Roy who lived in the High Street, Kenilworth. The Revd Roy rode to Westwood on a white pony and had a room in a house near the church. He appears to have been a great believer in the efficacy of wine and always kept a large stock in his room, ostensibly for the use of invalids. Revd Roy was a kindly man who believed whole-heartedly in education and set up a library in the village for adults and children that was still in use before World War One. He resigned the living because of ill health in 1871 and was followed by Revd Russell, who in 1877 was succeeded by the bizarrely named Revd John Octavius Coussmaker, known by the villagers as Mr Coachmaker.

The Revd Coussmaker was noted for his good nature and easy-going manner, and his lack of punctuality. On two occasions the congregation stood for an hour waiting for him to arrive. On the first occasion his excuse was that he had been removing a dead man from a ditch at the vicarage. On the second occasion he claimed to have been attacked by the vicarage bees and temporarily blinded.

Mary Dormer Harris's uncle was churchwarden at the church in the late 19th century. She wrote:

> *... had he not been in his accustomed place at the service, people would have expected the heavens to fall. Oh, oh! how the harmonium droned in those distant days! The congregation consisted of staid persons, who had mostly lived in the parish all of their lives, who did not marry or give in marriage, or run after enjoyment, but just stopped by their own firesides, in homely fashion, and were, I suppose content.*

Westwood Heath Road looking towards Westwood from Burton Green. Note how flat the landscape is here compared with the north of Coventry.

Esther Dash spoke to the *Coventry Evening Telegraph* (in 1998) of life in the village before World War One. She recalled:

Father was a farm worker and forester and mother did housework for the headmaster and made butter at the farm. Our lovely three bedroomed cottage had a large lawn to the front and a vegetable patch with apple, pear, damson and plum trees ... Each year the owner, Lord Leigh, would arrive on horseback to make his inspection, and award prizes for the best kept cottage and garden.

The old post office was a few doors away (and bears the crest of the Leighs). For 46 years it was run by Emma Smith, who finally retired at the age of 79. As a girl Esther remembered that the only other shop at Westwood was next to the smithy. Here she would buy sweets from Bumper Jones; while the smithy was always a favourite with children, who loved to watch the sparks fly. Esther recalled, 'George Duggins senior spent one half of the week at the little smithy in Westwood, and the rest of the week at the other in Duggins Smithy, a few miles away in Tile Hill.' She also remembered that the school (now the Greek Orthodox Church) was built in 1870. It had three teachers and the head's house was next to it. There was a flower garden for the girls and a vegetable plot for the boys. The big event of the year was Empire Day when Lord Leigh visited. The school was decorated and Lord Leigh was entertained by maypole dancing in the schoolyard, for which he rewarded the children by giving them the afternoon off.

Further Reading
Mary Dormer Harris, *Some Manors, Churches and Villages of Warwickshire.*
C.F. Neale, *The Church of St. John the Baptist, Westwood Heath*, 1944.

WHITLEY, PINLEY AND SHORTLEY

Whitley comes from the Saxon '*hwit ley*', meaning the white clearing, Pinley means 'Pinna's clearing' and Shortley means simply 'the short clearing'. All three were in the parish of St Michael.

Whitley was first mentioned in a grant by Ranulf, Earl of Chester, in the 12th century. He gave a chapel at Whitley to Coventry Priory. In 1219 the hamlet itself consisted of a chapel and three cottages. In 1250 Roger and Cecily de Montalt also gave grants to Coventry Priory but reserved the services of Walter Deyville and Miles Gerbod of Whitley. The hamlet grew over time and the manor passed through many hands, including the Bristows after 1428. John Bristow left the land to his son William, and the New Mill and other property to Edward. Both brothers were involved in lengthy disputes with the people of Coventry over common land, after fences they erected around common land were ripped down. The violent dispute was finally settled in 1482.

By 1574 the estate had passed to Bartholomew Tate, who became an MP for Coventry. In 1628 Zouch Tate sold the manor, which at the time included three watermills, to John Bowater. After Sir William Dugdale came here in 1658, he wrote, 'there only remains a manor house, with an old chapel and a mill, though it was formerly supposed to have been a village of divers inhabitants.' In 1774 it passed with the marriage of Jane, the daughter of Francis Wheler of Whitley Abbey, to Henry (later Lord) Hood. In 1867 Francis, 4th Viscount Hood, sold the estate to Edward Petre JP.

Whitley Bridge, which carried the original London Road across the Sherbourne and past Whitley Mill on the left. The mill and nearby cottage are now gone. (CCL)

Whitley Hall, demolished in 1953, may have been on the site of an older mediaeval building, although it is said to be of 17th-century origin. Charles I supposedly stayed there during the Siege of Coventry in 1642. This story may have real origins, for some writers of the past have confused Stoneleigh Abbey with Whitley Abbey. Charles did in fact stay at Stoneleigh, but it is not impossible that he also stayed at Whitley.

After 1808 Whitley Hall was enlarged in the Classical style and thereafter bore the name of Whitley Abbey, not through any monastic association but simply because of the popularity of the title. In 1874 there was a fire at the hall. The blaze was discovered shortly after 11pm, after the household had retired for the night. The servants in the west wing were forced to jump out of windows to safety. A horseman was sent to Coventry and in a short time the Sun Fire Brigade arrived. The newspaper reported that:

> *Just before reaching the cemetery the flames from the building could be seen reflected in the sky ... The spectacle presented on approaching the Abbey was singularly striking. The building seemed in a mass of flame.*

The west end of the building was almost entirely destroyed but the abbey was saved. It was said that this section of the building contained the remains of the older house, so the Abbey may have predated the 17th century. The damage led Edward Petre, who had previously built the Catholic chapel, to rebuild the west wing. He was also responsible for improving the grounds and planting Whitley Grove in a mediaeval quarry.

After Edward's death in 1902 his wife Lady Gwendaline and their son Oliver continued to live in the house. During World War One it was used for Belgian refugees and in 1924 it was sold by auction. The house was then derelict. The *Coventry Standard* sent someone to explore it in 1930, who wrote:

> *There was scarcely a pane of glass in the whole house, and this alone gave it a forlorn blind look. We climbed over a heap of plaster, and trod still firm floorboards beneath us into a long damp corridor, empty and echoing, and pierced along its length by doorways leading into empty rooms ... and all over it was the faint musty smell, that hangs so insidiously about a house that has known no warmth for a long time.*

In the grounds they found:

> *... the place of wild beauty ... with trees and shrubs in their full spring glory ... on the pool ... two swans floated, and as we approached came towards us ... they alone were the only living links with the former glory of the great house ... we went to the furthest end where an old quarry lay ... It was probably over two hundred years ago when this old quarry was made into a fern-lined grotto, with avenues and steps cut out of the solid rock ... It must have been a delightfully cool and shady retreat, with its miniature waterfalls and flower beds ... The shrubs, once so carefully trimmed, have grown until the pathways are choked ... No wonder the birds shun the place now, for little sunshine reaches the gloomy walks amid the moss grown rock.*

Whitley Abbey and its lake, photographed in 1912. (CCL)

Ray Holl MBE remembers Whitley Abbey from when he was a child. He and his friends saw a huge panelled door in the pool, which when it emerged was full of small carp swimming around in the deep recesses of the panelling. The Abbey and its grounds were eventually acquired by the Corporation, which demolished the house in 1953. In 1955 Whitley Abbey Comprehensive School opened on the site among the partly restored grounds.

The road to Whitley, the present London Road, was mentioned in the 12th century and was later called the Whitley Causeway. In 1723–4 the road was turnpiked and crossed the three-arched bridge built over the Sherbourne in the 18th century at Whitley Mill. A highway act of 1826–7 meant that a new stretch of road was laid north of the old one. The original road was diverted from Whitley Common and rejoined the old just above Willenhall Bridge. The old piece of the London Road, which originally ran over Whitley Bridge and past Whitley Mill and Abbey, was renamed Abbey Road. The deepness of the old road gives away its old name: the Hollow Way.

The original hamlet of Whitley was probably around Whitley Abbey and the mill area, while the later Whitley village was built in the 19th century on common land around the junction of the old and new London Roads. It consisted of buildings like Plemont Villa and the Royal Oak Inn, which was known as 'Ben Tedd's' because the licensee in 1861 was Benjamin Tedd. An older inn in Whitley was the Seven Stars near Willenhall Bridge, which was definitely used as an inn in the 18th century and later doubled as a farm.

Looking across Pinley Fields to Pinley House, with the Humber works at Stoke in the background. (CCL)

Whitley Common is actually common land attached to Coventry, not the manor of Whitley. The area of rough ground is now much smaller than it once was, having been enclosed in 1860 and 1875. Tom Burgess FSA, a 19th-century antiquarian, wrote in a paper on prehistoric discoveries in Warwickshire that, 'A camp which once existed on Whitley Common has long since been removed and no trace of its configuration has been preserved.' The earthworks were probably levelled out by unemployed weavers in the 1860s but the existence of a hollow way may suggest a prehistoric encampment that has since been forgotten. Ancient people certainly passed along the river, for up to the Charterhouse area prehistoric flints have occasionally come to light.

A Bronze Age axe-head was found in 1928 some distance away, about 500 yards from the old chapel at Whitley Abbey. Dating to around 1500 BC it was discovered lying on sandstone rock under three feet of soil. The area between Whitley and Baginton still contains some little explored land and some mounds which still exist may have prehistoric origins. One such mound survives on the present Whitley Common, on raised ground near the spinney by Leaf Lane (then Howe's Lane). This is the old circular gallows mound. The common was probably the site of the city gallows from the 17th to the early 19th century. Here robbers William Palliser, John Duplex, Margaret Brown and Sarah Jones, better known as the 'Coventry Gang', were hanged in 1763, followed by Thomas Summers for bestiality in 1784, Thomas Bissell, Richard Hawkins and John Farmer in 1785 and Mary Felkin in 1787, to name just a few. In 1821 Edward Bradshaw, alias 'Duckfat', was hanged in front of 10,000 people on the new drop gallows near the junction of the present Daventry Road. This new device, which broke the neck rather than strangling the criminal, was also used on Mary Ann Higgins in 1831. Her body hung on the gallows for two and a half hours while around 20 women rubbed the dead girl's hand on their necks to cure wens, or 'thick-neck' as it was called. For years after it was said that Higgins haunted the spot. One group of men went there at midnight and called out, 'Mary Ann, how are you?', to which a ghostly voice replied, 'wet and cold.' The men ran back to Coventry in terror only to be told that it was a joke!

The common was also a rendezvous for prize fighting. Ginger Berry and Harry Hodson of Longford fought here for five sovereigns a side in 1831. Ginger knocked Hodson out with the first blow and received the purse. In December 1836, Game One Shilton fought Whopper Flint for £10 a side. The press reported that 'the respectable company commenced operations, by making a roped ring, at the bottom of Whitley Common, near Howe's Lane, and not far from the spot where the malefactors are hanged.' The fight, which of course was illegal, was won after one hour by Shilton, leaving Flint to be carried away 'severely punished.'

The common also had military uses: troops were mustered here in 1745 and during World War Two unexploded bombs were brought here to be detonated. One bomb actually exploded while being lifted off the back of a truck. Martyn Hammond, then a young boy, recalled the occasion:

> One day in school we heard a large explosion which we knew to be a delayed bomb being set off on Whitley Common ... After school a group of us went to the common and walked around. It was a gruesome scene with bits of men hanging from trees and bushes, with parts of their uniforms and the lorry strewn all over. We were surprised that the area wasn't cordoned off and we children allowed to wander around. My brother picked up a piece of soldier's web belt and brought it home.

The brave crew of No.9 unit were buried in the London Road Cemetery and two posthumously received the George Cross.

A large area of the common was levelled in 1860 by unemployed weavers, after the trade collapsed in 1860. The largest remaining section was once part of a golf course laid out by the Coventry Golf Club and used until about 1912. After the war Billy Butlin, of holiday camp fame, who held part of the common, gave it to the city for playing fields. They were opened by the Duke of Edinburgh.

Just below the common on the London Road, the City Isolation Hospital, later Whitley Hospital, was opened. The hospital, described at the time as one of the finest in the country, was opened by the mayor of Coventry, Councillor Harris. It was officially opened in April 1934 and cost £113,500. After over 60 years of treating infectious diseases Whitley Hospital was finally demolished in the 1990s and houses and a supermarket were built.

Old Whitley only contained two farms, Coventry Old Park Farm, below the present common, and Whitley Abbey Farm near Whitley Abbey. The latter was acquired by the Government during World War One and German prisoners of war built an airfield known as Whitley Aerodrome there. After the war, the site was acquired by Armstrong–Whitworth, which had moved from Parkside. Here the

A drawing by Florence Weston of the now gone bridge across the Sherbourne at Shortley, below which stood the ancient floodgates of Charterhouse Mill. Nothing in this picture now remains.

company began producing Siskin fighters, which became the standard fighter for the Royal Air Force. In 1927 the company produced its second mass-produced aircraft, the Atlas biplane, and in 1929 its first airliner, the Argosy Mark II. On 17 March 1936 the first Whitley bomber took off from Whitley. This would become the first bomber to penetrate German airspace and was the workhorse of the RAF in the early years of World War Two. As the war continued AWA moved to a new site at Baginton and there continued production of the Whitley and other bombers such as the Lancaster.

Pinley, which stretches over towards Stoke Aldermoor, was open land until the early 13th century when Geoffrey Langley, son of its owner Walter de Langley, had an area of its woodland and moor land emparked with fence and ditch. In 1238 he built a house within the park, although this is likely to have been a rebuild for there was a chapel recorded there in 1222. Blyth, in his *History of Stoke*, records that in the 1870s at the southern extremity of Stoke Green, near the lane leading to the Aldermoor, stood an old cottage and dilapidated barn. The barn was all that remained of the old chapel. The south wall, he says:

> ... was tolerably perfect, having a couple of round headed lights at its eastern end, and just below them a mutilated stoup or piscina, with traces of a priest's door. The east end of the chapel was gone and its site occupied by a farm cottage. On the south of what appeared to be the chancel stood a substantial stone building of two storeys, the chimney pieces apparently of Tudor date.

This building he identifies as the priest's house. The manor of Pinley passed through many hands until it was sold to the Corporation in 1655.

Walter de Langley's manor house disappeared in the 15th century and its site was later referred to as Castle Close. Pinley House, the main building in the area after the loss of the manor house, probably dated from around 1700 and may have been built on the site of the original hamlet, which consisted of nine cottages in 1219. In 1822 it is recorded as standing in extensive parkland. It appears that after World War One Pinley House became the clubhouse of the Hillman Company and was later demolished and turned into the car park of Humber-Hillman. Attached to Pinley House was Pinley Fields or Round House Farm, which was all that remained of the original hamlet of Pinley. Other farms survived into the 19th and 20th century: Pinley or Aldermoor Farm, Pinley Green Farm

The Charterhouse in Shortley, originally a monastic house and later a private residence given to the city by Col. William Wyley.

and Pinley Hill Farm. Pinley Green must have once been an open space for in 1809 the Warwick Volunteer Cavalry twice mustered for inspection there. During the 19th century the area had many market gardens, nurseries and allotments. The land was built on at the end of World War One.

Shortley, although the name is no longer used, lay south of the present Gulson Road, bounded by Binley Road, Humber Road and Whitley. It appears that Shortley was originally known as Bisseley and belonged to Ranulf, Earl of Chester, who granted it to Liluph de Brinklow in the 12th century. The overlordship was later acquired by Robert de Montalt from whom it passed to Coventry Priory.

In the late 13th century Shortley was settled on Geoffrey de Langley. A manor house was built and belonged to John de Langley in 1489. The rest of Shortley was described as 'totally desolate and waste.' This was probably because the area lay close to the city walls, near two of the main entrances to the city. The land would need to be clear for defensive reasons.

After John de Langley died without an heir the estate was given to Edward Ringley, the second husband of John's widow. Ringley soon lost the manor after a lawsuit brought by the nieces of John de Langley, Alice Huntley, Isobel Skidmore and Christine Wigston, who held the manor from 1521. More suits followed before the manor was settled on William, son of Christine Wigston. In 1554 William sold the manor to his sister Katherine who was the wife of Edward Aglionby, later Recorder of Coventry and MP for Warwick.

In 1592 James Fitzherbert held the manor and in 1598 it was held by Edward Brabazon, whose family held it until 1634 when it was held by Issac Walden, former mayor and MP for the city. Before 1700 the estate was acquired by the Hopkins family of Foleshill, whose descendants held it into the late 19th century.

In 1381 William, Lord Zouch of Harringworth, bought 14 acres called Shortley Field and founded the Carthusian priory the Charterhouse. Work began under Robert Palmer, Procurator of the London Charterhouse, who became the first prior. It was said that Robert had had a vision in Jerusalem directing him to Shortley to build the monastery. The foundation stone of the church of St Anne, as it was known, was laid by Richard II in 1385 and he thereafter claimed that he and his queen had founded the church. He further endowed the order on condition that they maintained 12 poor scholars from seven years old, 'til they accomplish the age of 17 years, there to pray for the good estate of him the said king and his consort, during this life, and for the health of their souls after death.'

The order was founded as a rebellion against the larger, richer monastic houses. In Shortley the brothers lived a basic life, each having his own cell facing onto a square cloister walk. Talking was considered a unnecessary luxury and the house was noted for its strictness.

The order was run until the Dissolution and on 16 January 1539 the last prior, John Bouchard, surrendered the house to the Crown. Bouchard had buried the church plate in the ground, but it was returned to the Crown after Bouchard made a deal and gained a bigger pension than the prior of Coventry Cathedral.

Within months the buildings were dismantled, although parts of the church were still visible in around 1650 when the ground was levelled. The surviving remains (the present Charterhouse) date from the 16th and 17th century. After the Dissolution the building, which was originally open to the roof, had a second floor inserted. This floor cuts through a wall painting showing the crucified Christ above the Virgin, a centurion and a figure bearing the arms of the Langley family. The building passed through various hands and in 1848 was bought by John and Francis Wyley, chemists in Hertford Street. From 1889 it was occupied by William Wyley, later Col. Sir William Wyley, who left the house to the city after his death in 1940. The district of Shortley, except the Charterhouse land, was built upon from before World War One, changing from farmland to residential and factory units.

Shortley's most intriguing character is probably John de Nottingham, an alleged necromancer who in 1324 was hired by a group of notable Coventry and Warwickshire gentlemen to use his magic art to kill Edward II, the prior of Coventry and many others. To prove his art Nottingham killed Richard de Sowe using a waxen image and leaden pin through the head. When it became clear that the King was a target Nottingham's assistant William Mareschal broke and confessed the crime. The two men were taken into custody and a trial was held in Coventry Priory the following year. Nottingham could not tell his side of the story as he died in custody. Mareschal gave evidence, but the men that had hired them walked free. Mareschal then disappeared into the dungeons of Coventry and was never heard of again.

By Shortley once lay Bisseley, said by Dugdale to have been depopulated. Little else can be said of this lost village.

Further Reading
Iain Soden, *Excavations at St Anne's, Charterhouse, Coventry, 1968-87.*
Victoria County History, Vol. 8.
Various newspapers cuttings, Local Studies.
F.G. Fretton, *Whitley & Its Groves.*

WHITMORE PARK

Whitmore Park was originally known as Whitmoor, meaning 'the park on the White Moor'. This is said to have been because of the 'whitishness' of the ground. Dugdale describes Whitmoor in the 17th century as 'so moorish as that the ground would bear nothing but moss.' This moss was apparently white in one area, and could have been one of two species found on heath and moorland, *Cladonia macilenta* or *Cladonia coccifera*, both light-grey mosses that would seem white against the terrain. Another part of Whitmore was known as Black or Blakemoor, a name that could arise in an area of ferns where natural fires in hot summers charred the land. Another name connected to the area which may be Celtic in origin is the now gone Wyblyno Brook. This was fed by the Wyblyno Spring, which when measured in the 19th century was found to produce up to 100,000 gallons of water a day. The Springfield Brook, which runs through the lower end of Whitmore, now called Radford, was a large river in prehistoric times. It cut a valley through the area, where large river pebbles can still be found. One prehistoric stone tool and a worked flint have also come to light above the river valley in Beake Avenue.

In the 12th century land in Whitmore was owned by Robert Scot, Robert Beaufitz and Anketil Locard. The name Scot survived as Scots Hull, which became the Scotchill in modern times. Robert Scot probably had a hall there, possibly on or near the site of the later Whitmore Hall, which stood on the site of the present Whitmore Park School. The name Locard survived in the eastern boundary of the district as Lockyers or Lockhurst Lane.

By the 13th century Whitmore, consisting of wasteland and some arable, was in the hands of various freeholders including Geoffrey de Langley, Coombe Abbey and Coventry Priory. During

Munition workers, better known as 'Canary Girls', photographed at White & Poppe's during World War One. (CCL)

172

this period Coventry Priory began to acquire more of the land and in 1332 it obtained a licence to empark 436 acres of woodland and waste to form the manor of Whitmore Park.

In 1410 the area was described as having two houses, belonging to Roger Locard and Henry Beaufitz. There was also a building described as a lodge, which was the hunting lodge of the bishop and prior of Coventry, although it stood outside the entrance to the park and not in it (see Keresley). The park itself was elaborately fenced and ditched, its southern tip running from the Keresley/Radford Road up Sadler and Halford Lane across Penny Park Lane and along Park Gate Road, then in a southerly direction down Holbrook Lane and Lockhurst Lane. The south boundary of the park probably ran in a fairly straight line from the bottom of Sadler Road (formally Whitmore Park Lane), across to the bottom of Lockhurst Lane. Much of the lower section of the park is now known as Radford.

It appears that through its history there was always some arable land in the hunting park that was farmed by tenants, probably standing crops that could be easily ridden through. Deer would have been the main prey of the huntsmen, while other prey such as rabbits were caught by hawk. Many locals trespassed on the park, breaking down sections of the fence, much to the annoyance of the prior of Coventry, whose constant complaints were recorded in the Coventry Leet Book in the 15th century.

The park keepers and others associated with the maintenance of the park lived in the scattered hamlet of Park Gate or Penny Park Gate. Park Gate took its name from the north gate of the hunting park. It was at a house in Penny Park Gate that the press reported the capture of a murderer in 1776. One of the oldest surviving buildings there is the Parkgate Inn, which was recorded in 1750.

After the Dissolution the park came into the hands of Michael Camswell, who was probably a relation of the last prior, Thomas Camswell, who had been brought in to dissolve the priory. The acquisition of the lease by his family may have been a perk for this work. The park passed to Sir Ralph Sadler in 1547, who immediately passed it on to John Hales of Whitefriars, whose nephew built the New House (see Keresley) near the site of the hunting lodge. The manor remained with the Hales family until 1720, when it was sold to the Duke of Montagu. He sold it in 1722 to Richard Hill, who held the estate until 1806. In August 1807 the *Coventry Mercury* reported:

Whereas the Game on the Manor of Whitmore Park, belonging to the late John Lamb Esq, has been much destroyed by Poachers and other persons. Notice is hereby given, that a Game-Keeper is appointed, who is directed to prosecute all Persons found Trespassing, Shooting or Coursing on the said Manor.

By the mid-19th century the former hunting park had become mainly farmland, owned by individuals such as Hanson Lamb, John Alcock, Thomas Sheepshanks and John Hollick. The big house known as Whitmore Hall and 148 acres of the former park came into the hands of Edward Phillips. No images of this large building survive but it still stood in 1875 when a Miss Phillips was in residence.

Whitmore Hall may have stood on the site of an earlier mediaeval hall. It stood on the crest of the hill (on the site of Whitmore Park Infants School) facing the present Halford Lane, known in the mid-19th century as Straight Lane and Keepers Walk. It was probably a large Georgian house with

A visit by Queen Mary to White & Poppe's munition works in Whitmore Park on 18 September 1917. While there the Queen also visited various families in Colony and Munition Cottages.

a lawn in front crossed by a pathway and an avenue of trees running down the hill to the Hall Brook. Carriages would enter from a drive on the right of the building, which led to a semi-enclosed courtyard with outbuildings and stables. Straight pathways also led down the hillside among the trees and at the rear of the house were nearly 16 acres of open land.

A two-acre field separated Whitmore Hall from Whitmore Park Farm and cottage. They stood in nearly one and a half acres of ground and consisted of a long L-shaped building that faced the road and was approached by a drive which ran around the back of the building into a yard with an open barn for storing wagons. The last recorded inhabitants were Ernest and Edith Cox in 1939 and the cottage was occupied by Katherine and Ernest Plumber.

Another major farm was Grange Farm, which stood just above the present Radford Methodist Church on Beake Avenue. It was the largest farm complex in Whitmore Park (its site now stands in Radford) with a large farmhouse in open ground with an orchard and a huge square of stables and complex of farm buildings at the rear. The buildings ended at the Leg of Mutton Pond, named because of its shape. This large pond, also known as the Titty Bottle, was spring-fed and was always crystal clear and full of fish, a much-favoured place for watering the horses.

The age of the farm is uncertain but documents prove there was a farm called Grange Farm here in 1547, for it was recorded that '£12 8s 4d for the farm of the Grange or manor of Whitmore let to Michael Camswell, given in the first of Ed. VI, all priory land to Ralph Sadler.' The farm, entered from Sadler Road, is recorded in 1890 as being farmed by Arthur Sleath, who was still there in 1927. In 1929 N. Oakes took over, followed by Edward Burdett in 1931 and John Anderton in 1937. The directories have no reference to the farm in 1939–40, when it lay empty and awaiting demolition due to the extension of house building in Beake Avenue. However, the actual site of the farm was not built upon until 1952.

The land above Grange Farm was acquired before World War One by munition makers White & Poppe. The factory, the entrance to which was in Holbrook Lane, began by making engines for Morris cars. At the outbreak of war a contract was signed with Armstrong-Whitworth to produce bomb fuses. The mass-produced munitions were collected by train via a railway that entered the factory crossing what is now Burnaby Road. The trains stopped along a sunken track (which can still be seen) in front of warehouses that faced the present Beake Avenue. Behind was an area called the Dumps, where a number of semi-buried bunkers were used to store the finished product. One reason for these bunkers was the worry that pilots from the Radford Aerodrome would crash into the munition sheds as they persistently flew stunts over the factory, probably to impress the many girls inside.

During World War One the factory was staffed almost entirely by women known as 'Canary Girls' because of the effect of Tetrol staining their hands and faces. The girls would ladle the explosive, a yellow powder which when heated became a hot liquid, into shell cases and fuses. Girls were brought in from all over the country to keep up the war effort. In a letter written by the mother of Bob Ashmore we find out a little of the life of the 'Canary Girls' of 1917. She wrote:

> We have two Welsh girls living with us now, nearly everybody around us seem to have girl lodgers. They have turned out to be much nicer than expected ... The younger of the girls, Maggie, gets £2 18s a week and she is only 16. There has been a dreadful lot of accidents at W&P lately. Only this morning the magazine caught fire and we all sat here in the office waiting to be blown up. The girls were running down the lane for dear life in their overalls. On Wednesday a girl got her arm and half of her face blown off. She died yesterday.

The factory would eventually cover just over 114 acres and to keep up with the influx of workers work began on Munition Cottages and Whitmore Park Cottages. Over 400 wooden-framed cottages were built off Holbrook Lane around the factory and the strangely named Foleshill Park, which stands between Beake Avenue and Holbrook Lane, in the ancient Whitmore. These cottages, although temporary, were later sold by the Ministry of Defence to Coventry Corporation to be used as housing stock.

Part of the old White & Poppe factory was taken over in 1928 by Swallow Sidecars, created by William Lyons and William Walmsley in Blackpool. Austin Swallows were first produced here, followed by the Alvis Swallow, Fiat Swallow and Swift Swallow. In 1931 in conjunction with Standard the SS1 and SS2 were built and became the sensation of the 1932 Motor Show. The SS1 began the line of classics, which ended with the glorious 3½-litre SS100 with its long bonnet, huge headlights and runner boards. The partnership of Lyons and Walmsley split and in October 1933 a new company was formed called SS Cars Ltd, with William Lyons in sole control.

Working on chassis for the SS 100 series at SS Cars (later Jaguar) in Swallow Drive in the 1930s.

With his highly skilled engineers and designers, Lyons decided to build a new luxury car with a new name in 1935. He consulted an advertising agency and the name Jaguar was decided on. Permission to use the name had to be sought from Armstrong–Siddeley as they held rights to it, having used it for an aero-engine. The SS Jaguar Saloon was launched to the world in September 1935; it was followed by the SS Jaguar Tourer and the SS Jaguar 100.

During the war years SS did war work, producing 10,000 military sidecars, aero-engines and parts for Stirlings, Lancasters, Mosquitoes, Spitfires and refurbished and repaired Whitley bombers. Because of the war in Europe the SS name became unpopular and in April 1944 the Board of Trade gave the firm the go-ahead to change their name to Jaguar Cars Ltd, although the new name was not used until the war ended. Jaguars including the Mk 5 and the XK120 won much acclaim and in 1951–2 permission was sought to extend the factory towards Beake Avenue. This was not granted and production moved to Browns Lane, Allesley. The area was developed by Dunlop Aviation, who had occupied a large part of the site in different guises since before the war. During the war Dunlop produced, among other things, gun-firing systems for Spitfires, Hurricanes, Mosquitoes, Gladiators and Beaufighters, claiming in 1940 that every German plane shot down was destroyed using Dunlop firing systems.

Further Reading
The Victoria County History, Vol. 8.
Various newscuttings, Local Studies.
Andrews Newscuttings, Vol.1, 1895.
Nigel Thorley, *Jaguar in Coventry: Building the Legend*, Breedon Books, 2002.

WHOBERLEY

Historically most of Whoberley lay west of the Whorwell stream and was in the parish of Stoneleigh. The area has been farmland around the ancient moated Whoberley Hall for much of its history. It is first mentioned in around 1144 as 'Watburleia', which is believed to mean 'the wood or clearing belonging to Hwaetburh'. The name is Anglo-Saxon, making the site an ancient one. Hearsall Common became Whoberley Common, beyond Guphill Lane, also known as Whoberley Lane. Guphill probably comes from Roger Gupyll, who lived in Whoberley in 1274.

Oaks and beeches line the modern Guphill Avenue, which was originally the drive to Whoberley Hall. In 1975 Mr S. Langford told the *Coventry Evening Telegraph* that a lovely pair of iron gates once stood at the entrance to the drive. He remembered when the hall had become Whoberley Hall Farm, farmed by Fred Billing, after whom Billing Road is named. Fred sold much of his land to developers in 1928. In *Memories of Chapelfields and Hearsall*, Vol.2, Pauline Halsey recalls that she was born in newly built Glendower Avenue, which backed onto Whoberley Hall, the home of the Billingses. Glendower Avenue then had iron railings across it at the top of the hill and beyond was open countryside to the Allesley Old Road. She recalls:

> *Whoberley Hall was a beautiful old building with an oak panelled minstrel gallery and dining room … I remember Mr and Mrs Billing as a kind lady and gentleman who allowed we children from the new houses to play in their orchard. They always gave us fruit (the hall had a large grapevine) or sweets when our mothers sent us to buy eggs or milk from the farm dairy. In 1938 the farm was sold for housing development to take place and was demolished.*

Lyndale Road was cut first, but few houses were erected before war broke out. It then became a barrage balloon site and hostels were built to accommodate war workers, many of whom worked at the nearby Standard works.

A forgotten double-moated house belonging to William de Onley in 1250 once lay in the district near Canley. One of the Onley family was standard-bearer to Edward III when Calais was taken in 1347. His son John Onley was born in France and was twice mayor of Calais. On returning to England he became mayor of Coventry in 1396. The semi-waterlogged moats of the Onley residence could still be seen northeast of Moat House Cottages, Canley, in the late 19th century.

In 1687 James II came to Coventry from Lichfield. A group of 200 Whigs and Dissenters rode to Meriden to meet him while Sir Thomas Norton, the Deputy Lieutenant, with a party of Tories and churchmen, waited to greet him at Guphill Ford, which lay on the boundary of the city and county of Coventry. The ford was across the Sherbourne as it crossed the Allesley Old Road near the present Grayswood Avenue. Here Sir Thomas made a speech of welcome and accompanied the King to a civic greeting at Spon Bar Gates. After James II's forced abdication thousands of English, French and Dutch troops crossed the river here, followed by William of Orange, on their way to defeat Jacobite supporters in Scotland and Ireland.

Further Reading
Pauline Halsey, *Memories of Chapelfields and Hearsall*, Vol.2.
Victoria County History, Vol. 8.
Newspaper cuttings, Local Studies.

WILLENHALL

The earliest spelling appears to be 'Wilihale' (1195) from the Old English, '*welig-hale*,' meaning willow corner.

In Dugdale's revised history of Warwickshire, published in 1817, the village of Willenhall is described as being two miles from Coventry, with 22 houses and 126 inhabitants. Although not mentioned in Leofric's charter it belonged to the part of the district given by him to the monastery of St Mary in Coventry.

Dugdale's first mention of it is in a grant of free warren made to the monks of Coventry in the 41st year of the reign of Henry III. Dugdale reports that the name is written 'Wynhale' in that document. In another grant of 1260 it is written 'Wylenhal', which Dugdale believed referred to the many wells and springs that could be found here.

In 1279 the prior of Coventry held land here, with eight servants, two freeholders, six cottages and eight acres of wood. The main tenants were the Willenhall family who had a hall, a mill and a carucate of land. They were the principal tenants until the 15th century, and attended the prior's court in the village and later at Sow. After the Dissolution in 1539 the manor reverted to the Crown and was acquired by Sir Richard Lee, who sold it to John Hales, Clerk of the Hanaper and property speculator of Hales Place, Coventry. It passed to his nephew John Hales and continued in the Hales family until the 18th century. In 1720 it was sold to the Duke of Montagu, then Sir Richard Hill, after which it was passed on to Rowland Hill, remaining in the family until it was sold in 1807 to James Wyatt, who resided at Willenhall House.

There was an early chapel in Willenhall, dedicated to St James; this stood between the present Gunton Avenue and Knightlow Avenue, towards Dunsmore Avenue. Chapel Farm later occupied the site of the chapel, lying between the top of the present Chace Avenue (laid out 1931) and Gunton

Looking down St James's Lane from the London Road. This was the centre of the original village and the corner building, which is now gone, once held the post office. The building at the end is Willenhall School and beyond lay the brickworks. (CCL)

Part of Willenhall photographed from Toll Bar End in 1935. The buildings on the left stand around the junction of Stonehouse Lane. (CCL)

Avenue. It was described in the Coombe sale catalogue of 1923 as a dairy farm and farmhouse, 'nicely placed away from the road, and has been built near the site of an ancient building, known as St James's Chapel.' Of the chapel's history nothing is known.

During the 18th century the Seven Stars Inn was a stopping place on the turnpike road. It stood on the curve of the present Abbey Road (the original London Road to Toll Barr End). In August 1763 members of a London gang of roaming thieves met here before heading south to London. Four members failed to arrive, having been arrested for robbing the Castle Inn in Broadgate. These individuals, nicknamed the 'Coventry Gang', were hanged on nearby Whitley Common. By the 19th century the Seven Stars had become a farm and its remains are now the Folly Lane Club.

Manor Farm, also called Willenhall Hall, home of the Willenhall family, stood at the end of an avenue of chestnut and beech trees near the junction of the present Remembrance and Lysander roads and was originally the village's manor house. It was described in 1923 as a brick and stone 'Old Manor House' with farm buildings, three workers cottages, arable, meadow and pastureland. The manor house itself was described as being set in a garden and having an entrance hall, drawing room, dining room, breakfast room, five bedrooms, two attics, pantry, cellar, kitchen, back kitchen, dairy, old dairy, paved yard, wash house, baking oven and pump.

Willenhall House, built by the Hill family in around 1831, was set in over four acres of grounds off the London Road, a short distance above Willenhall Lane. In 1923 it was described as having a lounge hall, dining room, drawing room with ornamental glass panel, morning room, seven bedrooms, two servants' rooms, kitchen and servants' hall. Outside were stables, harness room and coach house and a four-roomed cottage set within pleasure grounds which contained tennis and croquet lawn, large kitchen garden stocked with fruit trees, orchard, tomato house, vinery, lean-to green house and a poultry shed.

The other main house of the once-rural village was the later 'Chace', built in 1897 by Dr Charles Webb Iliffe just before his retirement. Iliffe may have retired from doctoring, but he led an active life as a Tory MP for Coventry and served for 40 years as the county coroner. In 1930 the Chace became a hotel under the ownership of Gertrude Williams, who ran it until 1967. It is still a hotel.

The village of Willenhall and Tollbar End, which is in Willenhall, were part of the Coombe Abbey estate of the Cravens. Other parts of the village belonged to the Baginton Estate until 1918. This consisted mainly of a huddle of cottages at the junction of the London Road and Stonehouse Lane. Within this huddle stood Stone House Farm, built in 1687 by Thomas Viner, Willenhall Cottages, a pair of beautiful timber-framed thatched cottages, and a smithy worked by Mr Amos, the village blacksmith.

The charming thatched Willenhall Hall Cottages, which once stood in Willenhall on the London Road by Stone House Lane. When this photograph was taken in 1918 it was two separate cottages, home to Miss L.J. Cluley and Robert Bachelor.

Below Tollbar End were a small number of cottages, including Tollgate Cottage, belonging to the Coombe Abbey estate, and Ryton Tollgate Cottages, belonging to the Baginton estate. The tollgate itself stood at the London Road junction with Brandon Lane and in 1837 charged one penny per horse and sixpence for a vehicle. Its use came to an end in 1872 when an Act of Parliament abolished

Stone House Farm, Willenhall, in 1918. This was a farm that stood on land belonging to the Baginton estate. It consisted of more than 55 acres and was farmed at that time by Thomas Walker. It is now built over.

The Chace at Willenhall before it became a hotel. (CCL)

tollgates. The site of Tollbar End, Willenhall Hill, was considerably lowered and cut through in the 1830s. One small cottage can still be seen near the entrance to the shopping development standing high up on the original road level.

The Warr family lived at the tollhouse before World War One. Mr Warr recalled it in the late 1970s:

It was more or less a square building ... built on big sandstone foundations ... When I was born the front door was double doors so that the toll man ... could open the top one and look out ... Just opposite there were some posts left from the old gates and we put rope on these posts and we used to have that as a swing.

The London road itself was made with stones ... but when it came to the summer months, when it dried, it was very dusty ... The lane from the London road was known as Binley Lane, not St James's Lane ... it had hedges and trees at each side ... and it was narrow. There was only horse traffic using it so there was grass growing up in the middle ... The majority of workers in Willenhall were farm workers, and there were one or two gardeners. There was also the Willenhall Brickyard ... we sat in school and we would see the smoke coming out of the tall chimney at the brickyard. They made tiles, not bricks, though it was still called a brickyard and they made tiles which were sent away by rail, from what was known locally as Whitley Wharf.

The Chace National Service Hostel in Chace Avenue was erected on the site of Chapel Farm in 1941 as temporary housing for war workers from all parts of Britain. They later served as hostels for those seeking permanent homes in the city.

The Willenhall Wood Estate off St James's Lane, consisting of over 1,000 houses, was built in the late 1950s and early 1960s. This was the first council estate in Coventry to be built on the 'Radburn layout' (first used in America in the 1930s) in which houses were built overlooking greens with footpaths and garages at the back. It provoked much interest and won a national award in 1960. The rest of Willenhall was developed during the 1950s and 1960s, including the church of St John the Divine, built in 1955–7 and designed by Sir Basil Spence.

Further Reading

William Dugdale, *History of Warwickshire*, (1812 revised).

Kenneth Richardson, *Twentieth Century Coventry*, 1972.

The Coombe Abbey Estate sale catalogue, 1923.

The Baginton Estate sale catalogue, 1918.

WYKEN

Place-name experts seem confused by the origin of the name Wyken. It may come from the Saxon 'wic' for a dairy farm, or from the Old English 'wiken' meaning a dwelling, or 'wike' referring to a bend in the river. The 12th-century parish church of St Mary Magdalene is sited at the tip of a large bend in the River Sowe, which in the past was susceptible to floods.

The parish of Wyken, which has Caludon at its eastern tip, was first mentioned in the 12th century when its ancient church was among the chapelries granted to Coventry Priory by the Earl of Chester. The earliest known tenants on the estate were the Bruton or Bret family, who held much of it in the 12th and 13th century. They also held a water mill, and after the death of Walter Bret his widow gave it to the monks of Coombe Abbey for his soul. They did not hold it for long, since Walter de Langley acquired it from them for a yearly payment of white incense. The mill lay on the river down Croft Lane (now Wyken Croft) behind the church, below Wyken Bridge.

In the 13th and 14th century the principal holders of the estate were the Langley family and in the 16th century it came into the hands of the Willoughbys. Sir Francis Willoughby was forced to sell it to Richard Green and the estate remained in the Green family until around 1755, when the estate passed to William, later Baron Craven, of Coombe Abbey. His family held the estate until World War One when the Corporation acquired the land for housing.

Wyken Grange Farm, photographed by Arnold Stringer in the 1930s and demolished between the wars. It was originally called New House in 1834 and later became Wyken Grange. It stood near the present Torcross Avenue. (CCL)

A painting dating to 1800 of the church of St Mary Magdalene in Wyken Croft, said to have been built by Ranulf Gernon, Earl of Chester, and Thurstan Banaster, during the Baron's War. (CCL)

The Langleys may have had a house near a field called Hallfurlong, but the Willoughbys did not live in the area. The Greens' manor house, which dates to at least 1624, was probably Wyken House, now Manor Farm, which stands on the parish boundary on the Henley Road. In 1778 the tenant of the farm was William Sarjeaunt (it was known as Sarjeaunt's Farm), who also held the game rights of the manor. According to the *Victoria County History* the building's distance from the centre of Wyken suggests that it was probably the Greens' home before they acquired the manor and only became Wyken manor house afterwards. The original Manor House may have been nearer to the village centre on the site of Harris's Farm, which stood in Blackberry Lane. Tradition tells us that a member of the Craven family planted the first Wyken Pippin apple in the garden of this house.

There appears to have been a small settlement around the church and two mediaeval documents refer to rows of three houses. There were 23 houses in Wyken in 1279, but only 24 in 1563. By 1801 this had dropped drastically to only 12. The reduction in houses is believed to be because of enclosure, and many had disappeared by 1755.

The population later increased, mainly because of the sinking of a coal shaft below Sarjeaunt's Farm and the creation of the Craven Colliery, named after its owners, the Cravens of Coombe Abbey. The original shaft is thought to have been sunk in the 18th century and a new shaft sunk in the 20th century. By 1911 the population had reached 321; miners could also be found living in nearby Walsgrave and Potters Green. The Craven closed in 1927 because of problems caused during the 1926 General Strike.

The late George Smith of Walsgrave told me about the pit in the 1980s. He said:

> When you went down the pit bottom you come to what you call the weigh-head. Then you used to go down the first slant, 200 yards. You put a wooden thing under your arms and push along with your shoulders, you daren't put your arms out or you'd get them chopped off with the coal.

Another Wyken House stood near the present Wordsworth Road on the site of a 17th-century building belonging to Edward Clarke. It became known as Wyken House in the late 19th century. It was sold in 1929 and thereafter demolished and the land built upon. (CCL)

The late Bill Huckvale also spoke to me, and he recalled what happened next:

Manor House Farm or Sargeant's Farm, off the Bell Green Road but standing in the parish of Wyken, photographed in 1957. This is where tradition states the first Wyken Pippin apple was grown. (CCL)

Sheep on Henley Common, photographed in around 1911. (CCL)

Once down the shaft you had to walk downhill until you got to the slant where you and three others would get on the trolley, which would lower you down even deeper. Once at the bottom we got off and made our way to the stable to collect a pony ... The coal seam was about six feet thick and luckily there wasn't much gas or water about, the whole seam was at an angle slanting downwards. Roadways were cut deep into the ground and we had to work the seam back uphill. We had to supply tools and protective gear, also a cap and Davey lamp. The shafts were supported by pit props made of timber and they were quickly compressed into the floor by the immense pressure from above. Sometimes the floor would be pushed down so low that it had to be dug out again in the middle to get the ponies through.

Coal from the Craven would be taken to Coventry down the Walsgrave Road to the weigh-bridge. The late Percy Collins of Ansty Road told me, 'There was no houses along the road until you got to the weigh-bridge, it stood opposite the Walsgrave pub by Youell's Builders Office, that's where the weigh-bridge keeper lived'. After its closure the pithead was blown up in the 1930s.

The heart of the original small settlement and the site of the church of St Mary Magdalene is called Wyken Croft. The church, perhaps the most important in Coventry, has a rubble-built nave and chancel, part of the original building, which is believed to date to the year 1100. The only other addition since then has been the 15th-century church tower, with a spire added in the 17th century. In 1260 it is recorded that a priest was employed in the chapel to say Mass three times a week and at festivals.

Henley Mill in Mill Lane (now Henley Mill Lane), photographed before 1886 when it fell from use. A mill fed by the Sowe had stood here since the early 14th century. (CCL)

Inside the church is a Norman font and in 1957 a late 15th-century mural was discovered depicting St Christopher carrying the Christchild across the river. Outside the church until the 1960s was a grave known locally as the 'Pirate's Grave.' The story said that if you put your fingers in the eye sockets of the skull and crossbones on the stone and walked around it three times, the ghost of the pirate would appear. Later it was added that after walking around the stone three times one had to throw a stone through the church window. This practice brought about the removal of the stone altogether. The grave was not really a pirate's grave but a normal 17th to early 18th-century grave decorated with the skull and crossbones as a symbol of mortality. One unusual fact about Wyken church was told to me by an old miner from the Craven. He said that there are shafts running under the church and when it was dug the miners were told to leave the coal directly under the church in case of subsidence.

Wyken Pool or Slough is the largest expanse of water in Coventry and is believed to have been formed by mining subsidence in around 1860. In the 19th and through most of the 20th century it was a favourite fishing pool, where catches of one hundredweight of tench were not unusual. It is now surrounded by rough marshland and has been designated a local nature reserve.

Apart from its ancient church Wyken is famous for one other thing – the Wyken Pippin. It is said that Admiral Thomas Craven of the Cravens of Coombe Abbey brought an apple tree from Holland in around 1720 and planted it in the garden of the Manor House (Henley Road). It is said that the young tree flourished and produced beautiful fruit, which thereafter spread through the nation and was known as the Wyken Pippin. The *Gentleman's Magazine* of 1831 states that:

> *The original tree, a very old one, or the trunk of it with a strong sucker from its root, was growing in May 1827, at its native place, Wyken. The seed it is said was planted by a Lord Craven, who brought it from fruit he had eaten on his travels from France and Holland. All the cottagers round Wyken have from two to twelve trees each of this apple in their gardens, and it is a great favourite throughout the whole county of Warwick.*

The apple, which is now very rare, is small and stays green for a long time before turning yellow with patches of bronze. When picked in September—October the fruit is hard but on storage the yellow colour deepens and the apple become aromatic and superbly sweet and tender. It is at its best at Christmas but can be kept longer.

In Langford's *Staffordshire and Warwickshire*, published in around 1875, it is reported that the then --occupant of Wyken Manor House was William Henry Skelton Esq., and that the original apple brought from Holland by Admiral Craven was still in the garden.

Coventrian Les Ryan wrote in 1991:

> *I remember when blackberries grew in wild profusion in Blackberry Lane, Wyken. But that was more than sixty years ago. From the lane a narrow footpath led to the Miller's Brook, a local beauty spot, and thereby hangs a macabre tale and a true one. A Mr Ball who lived in Gun Lane, Stoke Heath, was jealous of his neighbour, Mr Rice. Mrs Ball and Mr Rice were suspected of having an affair. One afternoon, Mr Ball took time off from his work to confirm his suspicions. While the couple walked towards Miller's Brook, Mr Ball watched from the adjoining field. Then, from a gap in the hedgerow, Mr Ball shot Mr Rice dead. A local clergyman marked the spot where Mr Rice fell with a simple wooden cross and people came from miles around to gaze at the scene of this crime of passion.*

The late Abe Jepcott wrote in 1968 of his childhood memories of the same area.
> *This part of Wyken Croft with the river crossing the road was a magnet to us. Even the stones in the riverbed shone through the rippling water in pearly white, cinnamon and sovereign gold. There were no motor cars to bother us or spoil our fishing, but we did sometimes see a farmer's heavy waggon and horses crossing the shallow of the stream. The scene was real countryside from one end of Wyken Croft to the other ... On the other side of the old Wyken Church were many stretches of marshland and rivulets and pools overflowing from the river and in winter we often did some skating there when the water was frozen.*

Abe also recalled a huge tree near the present Lyng Hall School where the nightingale sang in the moonlight.

Mike Hancock of Wyken recalls his younger days in another part of Wyken.

We moved into 49, St Ives Road in the late summer of 1937. Just a few blocks had been built to the north side of the unmade road and we ate our first meal with plumbers and plasterers. Behind the house was one of Harry Green's farm fields. Potatoes growing at that time were replaced in later years by 'non harvestable by the locals' crops, wheat, oats and barley. At the rear of the house a path took us across the farm field and St Austell Road to a hedge which led down to the River Sowe, ideal for paddling and catching tiddlers, later perch, roach and other small fish. If we turned right up the Green Hill we found a pure spring of very palatable water, flowing down what is now The Drive.

On top of the hill were two very tall pine trees and beyond them the orchard of Stoke House. Across the fields and past the bottom spinney was Wyken Floods (now wrongly renamed Stoke Floods). The Green Hill was also wrongly renamed Stoke Hill again by officials who should have known better. We used to go bird nesting in the hedges around the floods and on more than one occasion were terrified that we would drown in the mud in our standard wartime footwear, wellies.

Later we formed St Ives Rovers and helped to make a cycle speedway track on the slope between St Ives road and Hipswell Highway. All this came to an end after the war, when the council went mad on building all around our part of Wyken ... As newly emerged adults the drinking holes were the Pippin and Wyken Club. The Wyken WMC was officially opened in two refurbished cottages for working men in 1935. Pippin had a good sized bar at the front and three small lounges, each with its own regular clientele, who never went into the other rooms. An original Wyken Pippin apple tree was growing at the rear of the Pippin pub and pre-war my mother took three twigs off it (with permission) and planted them in the garden, one survived and grew to a very large size.

Further Reading
Walsgrave History Project, *Walsgrave Remembered*, 1987.
Langford, *Staffordshire & Warwickshire*, 1875.
News cuttings, Local Studies.

Printed in Great Britain
by Amazon